Houston Astros 2020

A Baseball Companion

Edited by R.J. Anderson, Craig Goldstein and Bret Sayre

Baseball Prospectus

Craig Brown, Steven Goldman and David Pease, Consultant Editors
Robert Au, Harry Pavlidis and Amy Pircher, Statistics Editors

Copyright © 2020 by DIY Baseball, LLC.
All rights reserved

This book or any part thereof may not be reproduced or transmitted in any form or by any means, electronic or mechanical, including photocopying, recording, or by any information storage and retrieval system, without permission in writing from the publisher.

Limit of Liability/Disclaimer of Warranty: While the publisher and the author have used their best efforts in preparing this book, they make no representations or warranties with respect to the accuracy or completeness of the contents of this book and specifically disclaim any implied warranties of merchantability or fitness for a particular purpose. No warranty may be created or extended by sales representatives or written sales materials. The advice and strategies contained herein may not be suitable for your situation. You should consult with a professional where appropriate. Neither the publisher nor the author shall be liable for any loss of profit or any other commercial damages, including but not limited to special, incidental, consequential, or other damages.

Library of Congress Cataloging-in-Publication Data:
paperback
ISBN-13: 978-1-949332-74-2

Project Credits
Cover Design: Michael Byzewski at Aesthetic Apparatus
Interior Design and Production: Jeff Pease, Dave Pease
Layout: Jeff Pease, Dave Pease

Baseball icon courtesy of Uberux, from https://www.shareicon.net/author/uberux

Ballpark diagram courtesy of Lou Spirito/THIRTY81 Project, https://thirty81project.com/

Manufactured in the United States of America
10 9 8 7 6 5 4 3 2 1

Table of Contents

Statistical Introduction v

Part 1: Team Analysis

Houston Astros: Where Are You Going, Where Have You Been? 3
   Matthew Trueblood and Kevin Carter

Performance Graphs 7

2019 Team Performance 8

2020 Team Projections 9

Team Personnel 10

Minute Maid Park Stats 11

Astros Team Analysis 13

Part 2: Player Analysis

Astros Player Analysis 20

Astros Prospects 95

Part 3: Featured Articles

The Baseball Is Juiced (Again) 113
   Robert Arthur

The Moral Hazard of Playing It Safe 117
   Craig Goldstein

Index of Names 123

Statistical Introduction

Sports are, fundamentally, a blend of athletic endeavor and storytelling. Baseball, like any other sport, tells its stories in so many ways: in the arc of a game from the stands or a season from the box scores, in photos, or even in numbers. At Baseball Prospectus, we understand that statistics don't replace observation or any of baseball's stories, but complement everything else that makes the game so much fun.

What stats help us with is with patterns and precision, variance and value. This book can help you learn things you may not see from watching a game or hundred, whether it's the path of a career over time or the breadth of the entire MLB. We'd also never ask you to choose between our numbers and the experience of viewing a game from the cheap seats or the comfort of your home; our publication combines running the numbers with observations and wisdom from some of the brightest minds we can find. But if you *do* want to learn more about the numbers beyond what's on the backs of player jerseys, let us help explain.

Offense

We've revised our methodology for determining batting value. Long-time readers of the book will notice that we've retired True Average in favor of a new metric: Deserved Runs Created Plus (DRC+). Developed by Jonathan Judge and our stats team, this statistic measures everything a player does at the plate–reaching base, hitting for power, making outs, and moving runners over–and puts it on a scale where 100 equals league-average performance. A DRC+ of 150 is terrific, a DRC+ of 100 is average and a DRC+ of 75 means you better be an excellent defender.

DRC+ also does a better job than any of our previous metrics in taking contextual factors into account. The model adjusts for how the park affects performance, but also for things like the talent of the opposing pitcher, value of different types of batted-ball events, league, temperature and other factors. It's able to describe a player's expected offensive contribution than any other statistic we've found over the years, and also does a better job of predicting future performance as well.

There's a lot more to DRC+'s story, and you can read all about it in greater depth near the end of this book.

The other aspect of run-scoring is baserunning, which we quantify using Baserunning Runs. BRR not only records the value of stolen bases (or getting caught in the act), but also accounts for all the stuff that doesn't show up on the back of a baseball card: a runner's ability to go first to third on a single, or advance on a fly ball.

Defense

Where offensive value is *relatively* easy to identify and understand, defensive value is...not. Over the past dozen years, the sabermetric community has focused mostly on stats based on zone data: a real-live human person records the type of batted ball and estimated landing location, and models are created that give expected outs. From there, you can compare fielders' actual outs to those expected ones. Simple, right?

Unfortunately, zone data has two major issues. First, zone data is recorded by commercial data providers who keep the raw data private unless you pay for it. (All the statistics we build in this book and on our website use public data as inputs.) That hurts our ability to test assumptions or duplicate results. Second, over the years it has become apparent that there's quite a bit of "noise" in zone-based fielding analysis. Sometimes the conclusions drawn from zone data don't hold up to scrutiny, and sometimes the different data provided by different providers don't look anything alike, giving wildly different results. Sometimes the hard-working professional stringers or scorers might unknowingly inflict unconscious bias into the mix: for example good fielders will often be credited with more expected outs despite the data, and ballparks with high press boxes tend to score more line drives than ones with a lower press box.

Enter our Fielding Runs Above Average (FRAA). For most positions, FRAA is built from play-by-play data, which allows us to avoid the subjectivity found in many other fielding metrics. The idea is this: count how many fielding plays are made by a given player and compare that to expected plays for an average fielder at their position (based on pitcher ground ball tendencies and batter handedness). Then we adjust for park and base-out situations.

When it comes to catchers, our methodology is a little different thanks to the laundry list of responsibilities they're tasked with beyond just, well, catching and throwing the ball. By now you've probably heard about "framing" or the art of making umpires more likely to call balls outside the strike zone for strikes. To put this into one tidy number, we incorporate pitch tracking data (for the years it exists) and adjust for important factors like pitcher, umpire, batter and home-field advantage using a mixed-model approach. This grants us a number for how many strikes the catcher is personally adding to (or subtracting from) his pitchers' performance...which we then convert to runs added or lost using linear weights.

Framing is one of the biggest parts of determining catcher value, but we also take into account blocking balls from going past, whether a scorer deems it a passed ball or a wild pitch. We use a similar approach—one that really benefits from the pitch tracking data that tells us what ends up in the dirt and what doesn't. We also include a catcher's ability to prevent stolen bases and how well they field balls in play, and *finally* we come up with our FRAA for catchers.

Pitching

Both pitching and fielding make up the half of baseball that isn't run scoring: run prevention. Separating pitching from fielding is a tough task, and most recent pitching analysis has branched off from Voros McCracken's famous (and controversial) statement, "There is little if any difference among major-league pitchers in their ability to prevent hits on balls hit in the field of play." The research of the analytic community has validated this to some extent, and there are a host of "defense-independent" pitching measures that have been developed to try and extract the effect of the defense behind a hurler from the pitcher's work.

Our solution to this quandary is Deserved Run Average (DRA), our core pitching metric. DRA looks like earned run average (ERA), the tried-and-true pitching stat you've seen on every baseball broadcast or box score from the past century, but it's very different. To start, DRA takes an event-by-event look at what the pitchers does, and adjusts the value of that event based on different environmental factors like park, batter, catcher, umpire, base-out situation, run differential, inning, defense, home field advantage, pitcher role and temperature. That mixed model gives us a pitcher's expected contribution, similar to what we do for our DRC+ model for hitters and FRAA model for catchers. (Oh, and we also consider the pitcher's effect on basestealing and on balls getting past the catcher.)

It's important to note that DRA is set to the scale of runs allowed per nine innings (RA9) instead of ERA, which makes DRA's scale slightly higher than ERA's. The reason for this is because ERA tends to overrate three types of pitchers:

1. Pitchers who play in parks where scorers hand out more errors. Official scorers differ significantly in the frequency at which they assign errors to fielders.
2. Ground-ball pitchers, because a substantial proportion of errors occur on groundballs.
3. Pitchers who aren't very good. Better pitchers often allow fewer unearned runs than bad pitchers, because good pitchers tend to find ways to get out of jams.

Since the last time you picked up an edition of this book, we've also made a few minor changes to DRA to make it better. Recent research into "tunneling"—the act of throwing consecutive pitches that appear similar from a batter's point of view until after the swing decision point–data has given us a new contextual factor to account for in DRA: plate distance. This refers to the distance between successive pitches as they approach the plate, and while it has a smaller effect than factors like velocity or whiff rate, it still can help explain pitcher strikeout rate in our model.

New Pitching Metrics for 2020

We're including a few "new" pitching metrics in the book for the 2020 edition, though unlike last year, these numbers may be a little bit more familiar to those of you who have spent some time investigating baseball statistics.

Fastball Percentage

Our fastball percentage (FB%) statistic measures how frequently a pitcher throws a pitch classified as a "fastball," measured as a percentage of overall pitches thrown. We qualify three types of fastballs:

1. The traditional four-seam fastball;
2. The two-seam fastball or sinker;
3. "Hard cutters," which are pitches that have the movement profile of a cut fastball and are used as the pitcher's primary offering or in place of a more traditional fastball.

For example, a pitcher with a FB% of 67 throws any combination of these three pitches about two-thirds of the time.

Whiff Rate

Everybody loves a swing and a miss, and whiff rate (WHF) measures how frequently pitchers induce a swinging strike. To calculate WHF, we add up all the pitches thrown that ended with a swinging strike, then divide that number by a pitcher's total pitches thrown. Most often, high whiff rates correlate with high strikeout rates (and overall effective pitcher performance).

Called Strike Probability

Called Strike Probability (CSP) is a number that represents the likelihood that all of a pitcher's pitches will be called a strike while controlling for location, pitcher and batter handedness, umpire and count. Here's how it works: on each pitch, our model determines how many times (out of 100) that a similar pitch was called for a strike given those factors mentioned above, and when normalized for each batter's strike zone. Then we average the CSP for all pitches thrown by a pitcher in a season, and that gives us the yearly CSP percentage you see in the stats boxes.

As you might imagine, pitchers with a higher CSP are more likely to work in the zone, where pitchers with a lower CSP are likely locating their pitches outside the normal strike zone, for better or for worse.

Projections

Many of you aren't turning to this book just for a look at what a player has done, but for a look at what a player is going to do: the PECOTA projections. PECOTA, initially developed by Nate Silver (who has moved on to greater fame as a political analyst), consists of three parts:

1. Major-league equivalencies, which use minor-league statistics to project how a player will perform in the major leagues;
2. Baseline forecasts, which use weighted averages and regression to the mean to estimate a player's current true talent level; and
3. Aging curves, which uses the career paths of comparable players to estimate how a player's statistics are likely to change over time.

With all those important things covered, let's take a look at what's in the book this year.

Team Prospectus

Most of this book is composed of team chapters, with one for each of the 30 major-league franchises. On the first page of each chapter, you'll see a box that contains some of the key statistics for each team as well as a very inviting stadium diagram. (You can see an example of this for the Milwaukee Brewers on this very page!)

We start with the team name, their unadjusted 2019 win-loss record, and their divisional ranking. Beneath that are a host of other team statistics. **Pythag** presents an adjusted 2019 winning percentage, calculated by taking runs scored per game (**RS/G**) and runs allowed per game (**RA/G**) for the team, and running them through a version of Bill James' Pythagorean formula that was refined and improved by David Smyth and Brandon Heipp. (The formula is called "Pythagenpat," which is equally fun to type and to say.)

Next up is **DRC+**, described earlier, to indicate the overall hitting ability of the team either above or below league-average. Run prevention on the pitching side is covered by **DRA** (also mentioned earlier) and another metric: Fielding Independent Pitching (**FIP**), which calculates another ERA-like statistic based on strikeouts, walks, and home runs recorded. Defensive Efficiency Rating (**DER**) tells us the percentage of balls in play turned into outs for the team, and is a quick fielding shorthand that rounds out run prevention.

After that, we have several measures related to roster composition, as opposed to on-field performance. **B-Age** and **P-Age** tell us the average age of a team's batters and pitchers, respectively. **Salary** is the combined team payroll for all on-field players, and Doug Pappas' Marginal Dollars per Marginal Win (**M$/MW**) tells us how much money a team spent to earn production above replacement level.

Ending this batch of statistics is the number of disabled list days a team had over the season (**IL Days**) and the amount of salary paid to players on the disabled list (**$ on IL**); this final number is expressed as a percentage of total payroll.

Next to each of these stats, we've listed each team's MLB rank in that category from first to 30th. In this, first always indicates a positive outcome and 30th a negative outcome, except in the case of salary—first is highest.

After the franchise statistics, we share a few items about the team's home ballpark. There's the aforementioned diagram of the park's dimensions (including distances to the outfield wall), a graphic showing the height of the wall from the left-field pole to the right-field pole, and a table showing three-year park factors for the stadium. The park factors are displayed as indexes where 100 is average, 110 means that the park inflates the statistic in question by 10 percent, and 90 means that the park deflates the statistic in question by 10 percent.

On the second page of each team chapter, you'll find three graphs. The first is the **2019 Hit List Ranking**. This shows our Hit List Rank for the team on each day of the 2019 season and is intended to give you a picture of the ups and downs of the team's season. Hit List Rank measures overall team performance and drives the Hit List Power Rankings at the baseballprospectus.com website.

The second graph is **Committed Payroll** and helps you see how the team's payroll has compared to the MLB and divisional average payrolls over time. Payroll figures are current as of January 1, 2020; with so many free agents still unsigned as of this writing, the final 2020 figure will likely be significantly different for many teams. (In the meantime, you can always find the most current data at Baseball Prospectus' Cot's Baseball Contracts page.)

The third graph is **Farm System Ranking** and displays how the Baseball Prospectus prospect team has ranked the organization's farm system since 2007.

After the graphs, we have a **Personnel** section that lists many of the important decision-makers and upper-level field and operations staff members for the franchise, as well as any former Baseball Prospectus staff members who are currently part of the organization. (In very rare circumstances, someone might be on both lists!)

Juan Soto LF

Born: 10/25/98 Age: 21 Bats: L Throws: L
Height: 6'1" Weight: 185 Origin: International Free Agent, 2015

YEAR	TEAM	LVL	AGE	PA	R	2B	3B	HR	RBI	BB	K	SB	CS	AVG/OBP/SLG
2017	NAT	RK	18	27	3	1	1	0	4	2	1	0	0	.320/.370/.440
2017	HAG	A	18	96	15	5	0	3	14	10	8	1	2	.360/.427/.523
2018	HAG	A	19	74	12	5	3	5	24	14	13	2	0	.373/.486/.814
2018	POT	A+	19	73	17	3	1	7	18	11	8	0	1	.371/.466/.790
2018	HAR	AA	19	35	4	2	0	2	10	4	7	1	0	.323/.400/.581
2018	WAS	MLB	19	494	77	25	1	22	70	79	99	5	2	.292/.406/.517
2019	WAS	MLB	20	659	110	32	5	34	110	108	132	12	1	.282/.401/.548
2020	WAS	MLB	21	630	92	30	3	35	102	85	123	5	2	.284/.382/.543

Comparables: Ronald Acuña Jr., Mike Trout, Tony Conigliaro

YEAR	TEAM	LVL	AGE	PA	DRC+	VORP	BABIP	BRR	FRAA	WARP
2017	NAT	RK	18	27	135	1.5	.333	0.0	RF(9): -1.1	0.0
2017	HAG	A	18	96	181	8.0	.373	1.0	RF(19): -1.9, LF(2): -0.3	0.9
2018	HAG	A	19	74	222	14.5	.405	0.3	RF(14): 1.1, CF(2): 0.2	1.2
2018	POT	A+	19	73	260	15.4	.340	1.4	RF(14): 1.0, LF(1): 0.0	1.6
2018	HAR	AA	19	35	113	3.6	.364	0.0	LF(4): 0.6, RF(4): -0.5	0.1
2018	WAS	MLB	19	494	125	40.5	.338	-0.5	LF(114): 2.7	3.0
2019	WAS	MLB	20	659	136	49.0	.312	1.4	LF(150): -0.8	4.9
2020	WAS	MLB	21	630	133	43.6	.310	-0.1	LF 3	4.8

Position Players

After all that information and a thoughtful bylined essay covering each team, we present our player comments. These are also bylined, but due to frequent franchise shifts during the offseason, our bylines are more a rough guide than a perfect accounting of who wrote what.

Each player is listed with the major-league team that employed him as of early January 2020. If a player changed teams after that point via free agency, trade, or any other method, you'll be able to find them in the chapter for their previous squad.

As an example, take a look at the player comment for Nationals outfielder Juan Soto: the stat block that accompanies his written comment is at the top of this page. First we cover biographical information (age is as of June 30, 2020) before moving onto the stats themselves. Our statistic columns include standard identifying information like **YEAR**, **TEAM**, **LVL** (level of affiliated play) and **AGE** before getting into the numbers. Next, we provide raw, untranslated numbers like you might find on the back of your dad's baseball cards: **PA** (plate appearances), **R** (runs), **2B** (doubles), **3B** (triples), **HR** (home runs), **RBI** (runs batted in), **BB** (walks), **K** (strikeouts), **SB** (stolen bases) and **CS** (caught stealing).

Next, we have unadjusted "slash" statistics: **AVG** (batting average), **OBP** (on-base percentage) and **SLG** (slugging percentage). Following the slash line is **DRC+** (Deserved Runs Created Plus), which we described earlier as total offensive expected contribution compared to the league average.

One of our oldest active metrics, **VORP** (Value Over Replacement Player), considers offensive production, position and plate appearances. In essence, it is the number of runs contributed beyond what a replacement-level player at the same position would contribute if given the same percentage of team plate appearances. VORP does not consider the quality of a player's defense.

BABIP (batting average on balls in play) tells us how often a ball in play fell for a hit, and can help us identify whether a batter may have been lucky or not...but note that high BABIPs also tend to follow the great hitters of our time, as well as speedy singles hitters who put the ball on the ground.

The next item is **BRR** (Baserunning Runs), which covers all of a player's baserunning accomplishments including (but not limited to) swiped bags and failed attempts. Next is **FRAA** (Fielding Runs Above Average), which also includes the number of games previously played at each position noted in parentheses. Multi-position players have only their two most frequent positions listed here, but their total FRAA number reflects all positions played.

Our last column here is **WARP** (Wins Above Replacement Player). WARP estimates the total value of a player, which means for hitters it takes into account hitting runs above average (calculated using the DRC+ model), BRR and FRAA. Then, it makes an adjustment for positions played and gives the player a credit for plate appearances based upon the difference between "replacement level"—which is derived from the quality of players added to a team's roster after the start of the season–and the league average.

The final line just below the stats box is **PECOTA** data, which is discussed further in a following section.

Catchers

Catchers are a special breed, and thus they have earned their own separate box which displays some of the defensive metrics that we've built just for them. As an example, let's check out J.T. Realmuto.

The **YEAR** and **TEAM** columns match what you'd find in the other stat box. **P. COUNT** indicates the number of pitches thrown while the catcher was behind the plate, including swinging strikes, fouls and balls in play. **FRM RUNS** is the total run value the catcher provided (or cost) his team by influencing the umpire to call strikes where other catchers did not. **BLK RUNS** expresses the total run value above or below average for the catcher's ability to prevent wild pitches and passed balls. **THRW RUNS** is calculated using a similar model as the previous two statistics, and it measures a catcher's ability to throw out basestealers but also to dissuade them from testing his arm in the first place. It takes into account factors like the pitcher (including his delivery and pickoff move) and baserunner (who could be as fast as Billy Hamilton or as slow as Yonder Alonso). **TOT RUNS** is the sum of all of the previous three statistics.

Justin Verlander RHP
Born: 02/20/83 Age: 37 Bats: R Throws: R
Height: 6'5" Weight: 225 Origin: Round 1, 2004 Draft (#2 overall)

YEAR	TEAM	LVL	AGE	W	L	SV	G	GS	IP	H	HR	BB/9	K/9	K	GB%	BABIP
2017	DET	MLB	34	10	8	0	28	28	172	153	23	3.5	9.2	176	34%	.283
2017	HOU	MLB	34	5	0	0	5	5	34	17	4	1.3	11.4	43	32%	.194
2018	HOU	MLB	35	16	9	0	34	34	214	156	28	1.6	12.2	290	31%	.272
2019	HOU	MLB	36	21	6	0	34	34	223	137	36	1.7	12.1	300	36%	.219
2020	HOU	MLB	37	15	6	0	29	29	184	138	28	2.3	12.1	248	35%	.274

Comparables: Zack Greinke, A.J. Burnett, Aníbal Sánchez

YEAR	TEAM	LVL	AGE	WHIP	ERA	DRA	WARP	MPH	FB%	WHF	CSP
2017	DET	MLB	34	1.28	3.82	4.03	3.0	97.7	58	11	47.8
2017	HOU	MLB	34	0.65	1.06	3.08	0.9	97.5	59.6	15.1	49.9
2018	HOU	MLB	35	0.90	2.52	2.33	7.3	97.5	61.2	16.2	51.6
2019	HOU	MLB	36	0.80	2.58	2.51	7.9	96.8	49.9	17.5	48.3
2020	HOU	MLB	37	1.01	2.75	2.95	5.3	95.8	54.6	15.1	48.2

Pitchers

Let's give our pitchers a turn, using 2019 AL Cy Young winner Justin Verlander as our example. Take a look at his stat block: the first line and the **YEAR**, **TEAM**, **LVL** and **AGE** columns are the same as in the position player example earlier.

Here too, we have a series of columns that display raw, unadjusted statistics compiled by the pitcher over the course of a season: **W** (wins), **L** (losses), **SV** (saves), **G** (games pitched), **GS** (games started), **IP** (innings pitched), **H** (hits allowed) and **HR** (home runs allowed). Next we have two statistics that are rates: **BB/9** (walks per nine innings) and **K/9** (strikeouts per nine innings), before returning to the unadjusted K (strikeouts).

Next up is **GB%** (ground ball percentage), which is the percentage of all batted balls that were hit on the ground, including both outs and hits. Remember, this is based on observational data and subject to human error, so please approach this with a healthy dose of skepticism.

BABIP (batting average on balls in play) is calculated using the same methodology as it is for position players, but it often tells us more about a pitcher than it does a hitter. With pitchers, a high BABIP is often due to poor defense or bad luck, and can often be an indicator of potential rebound, and a low BABIP may be cause to expect performance regression. (A typical league-average BABIP is close to .290-.300.)

The metrics **WHIP** (walks plus hits per inning pitched) and **ERA** (earned run average) are old standbys: WHIP measures walks and hits allowed on a per-inning basis, while ERA measures earned runs on a nine-inning basis. Neither of these stats are translated or adjusted.

DRA (Deserved Run Average) was described at length earlier, and measures how many runs the pitcher "deserved" to allow per nine innings. Please note that since we lack all the data points that would make for a "real" DRA for minor-league events, the DRA displayed for minor league partial-seasons is based off of different data. (That data is a modified version of our cFIP metric, which you can find more information about on our website.)

Just like with hitters, **WARP** (Wins Above Replacement Player) is a total value metric that puts pitchers of all stripes on the same scale as position players. We use DRA as the primary input for our calculation of WARP. You might notice that relief pitchers (due to their limited innings) may have a lower WARP than you were expecting or than you might see in other WARP-like metrics. WARP does not take leverage into account, just the actions a pitcher performs and the expected value of those actions...which ends up judging high-leverage relief pitchers differently than you might imagine given their prestige and market value.

MPH gives you the pitcher's 95th percentile velocity for the noted season, in order to give you an idea of what the *peak* fastball velocity a pitcher possesses. Since this comes from our pitch-tracking data, it is not publicly available for minor-league pitchers.

Finally, we display the three new pitching metrics we described earlier. **FB%** (fastball percentage) gives you the percentage of fastballs thrown out of all pitches. **WHF** (whiff rate) tells you the percentage of swinging strikes induced out of all pitches. **CSP** (called strike probability) expresses the likelihood of all pitches thrown to result in a called strike, after controlling for factors like handedness, umpire, pitch type, count and location.

PECOTA

All players have PECOTA projections for 2020, as well as a set of other numbers that describe the performance of comparable players according to PECOTA. All projections for 2020 are for the player at the date we went to press in early January and are projected into the league and park context as indicated by the team abbreviation. (Note that players at very low levels of the minors are too unpredictable to assess using these numbers.) All PECOTA projected statistics represent a player's projected major-league performance.

Below the projections are the player's three highest-scoring comparable players as determined by PECOTA. All comparables represent a snapshot of how the listed player was performing at the same age as the current player, so if a

23-year-old pitcher is compared to Bartolo Colón, he's actually being compared to a 23-year-old Colón, not the version that pitched for the Rangers in 2018, nor to Colón's career as a whole.

A few points about pitcher projections. First, we aren't yet projecting peak velocity, so that column will be blank in the PECOTA lines. Second, projecting DRA is trickier than evaluating past performance, because it is unclear how deserving each pitcher will be of his anticipated outcomes. However, we know that another DRA-related statistic–contextual FIP or cFIP–estimates future run scoring very well. So for PECOTA, the projected DRA figures you see are based on the past cFIPs generated by the pitcher and comparable players over time, along with the other factors described above.

Lineouts

In each chapter's Lineouts section, you'll find abbreviated text comments, as well as all the same information you'd find in our full player comments. The only difference is that we limit the stats boxes in this section to only including the 2019 information for each player.

Managers

After all those wonderful team chapters, we've got statistics for each big-league manager, all of whom are organized by alphabetical order. Here you'll find a block including an extraordinary amount of information collected from each manager's entire career. For more information on the acronyms and what they mean, please visit the Glossary at www.baseballprospectus.com.

There is one important metric that we'd like to call attention to, and you'll find it next to each manager's name: **wRM+** (weighted reliever management plus). Developed by Rob Arthur and Rian Watt, wRM+ investigates how good a manager is at using their best relievers during the moments of highest leverage, using both our proprietary DRA metric as well as Leverage Index. wRM+ is scaled to a league average of 100, and a wRM+ of 105 indicates that relievers were used approximately five percent "better" than average. On the other hand, a wRM+ of 95 would tell us the team used its relievers five percent "worse" than the average team.

While wRM+ does not have an extremely strong correlation with a manager, it is statistically significant; this means that a manager is not *entirely* responsible for a team's wRM+, but does have some effect on that number.

PECOTA Leaderboards

If you're familiar with PECOTA, then you'll have noticed that the projection system often appears bullish on players coming off a bad year and bearish on players coming off a good year. (This is because the system weights several previous seasons, not just the most recent one.) In addition, we publish the 50th

Houston Astros 2020

percentile projections for each player–which is smack in the middle of the range of projected production—which tends to mean PECOTA stat lines don't often have extreme results like 40 home runs or 250 strikeouts in a given season. In essence, PECOTA doesn't project very many extreme seasons.

At the end of the book, we've ranked the top players at each position based on their PECOTA projections. This might help you visualize just how a given player's projection compares to that of their peers, so that even if a dramatic stat line isn't projected, you can still imagine how they stack up against the rest of the league.

Part 1: Team Analysis

Houston Astros: Where Are You Going, Where Have You Been?

Matthew Trueblood and Kevin Carter

2019: What Went Right

Before the fall, used as a verb, not a noun—which is to say the commissioner's report: Squarely in the sweet spot of a dynastic window, the Astros entered 2019 expecting to be exactly where they ended up. Their ideal campaign was merely one that didn't go catastrophically wrong, and they managed precisely that. Undeniably, however, they also got some things even more right than they had reason to expect. Alex Bregman continued his development and assault on American League pitching as he produced an 8.6 WARP season, second only to Mike Trout in the majors. Not only did he rake at the plate (157 DRC+), but he slid over and played a capable shortstop when Carlos Correa landed on the shelf during the season. He finished second to Trout in the MVP balloting, and there's a reasonable argument to be made for his having won it. Yordan Alvarez posted a 149 DRC+, good for seventh-best among batters who went to the plate at least 300 times. Even a starry-eyed Alvarez booster would have pegged him for a bit less production than that.

It can't get much better than Gerrit Cole and Justin Verlander. In his platform season, Cole absolutely took off, recording a 2.36 DRA to go with a paltry 49 DRA-. He led the majors in strikeouts (326) and strikeouts per nine (13.8) and the AL in ERA (2.50). He looked like the prototype of what a pitcher should be, except advanced beyond reason. Verlander continued to shine at age 36. The old-schooler that he is, he paced the majors in wins (21), innings pitched (223), WHIP (0.803), and hits per nine (5.5), and led the AL in strikeout to walk ratio. His big bugaboo was the longball—he surrendered 36 home runs in 2019, more than one per start. The damage was limited thanks to his stinginess with baserunners, and he netted out a 2.51 DRA for his efforts, good for sixth in the majors and second only to Cole in the American League.

The back end of the starting rotation, fairly discussed as a potential weakness prior to the season, turned out to be solid. Wade Miley gave Houston four good months to open the season. Old friends Brad Peacock and Collin McHugh helped stabilize things in their familiar swingman roles, and Corbin Martin (though he would finish with ugly numbers and underwent Tommy John surgery during the summer) impressed enough to put himself on the radar as a July trade chip.

The real revelations in the rotation, though, were Zack Greinke, whom the team acquired under the wire at the trade deadline for a package that included Martin, and José Urquidy, whose heroism carried all the way into the World Series. Urquidy's command of four pitches should be enough to push him into the 2020 rotation. In the bullpen, Roberto Osuna and Ryan Pressly formed one of the league's most formidable back-end duos, and Josh James took a huge step forward, emerging as more than a short-burst, fastball-first guy. Will Harris, who might be the most underrated reliever in baseball, was brilliant as usual.

2019: What Went Wrong

Robinson Chirinos was the competent hitter the team hoped they were adding when they signed him over the winter, but isn't a long-term solution behind the plate. No such long-term answer emerged in 2019. Correa and José Altuve both endured protracted struggles related to injuries that took them off the field for a while, and that clearly affected them even while they played through them at other times. Each poses a bit more risk going forward than their talent and track records dictate. Miley regressed nightmarishly late in the season, and had to be left off the roster after the ALDS. Forrest Whitley, persistently hailed as an elite prospect, pitched poorly and was unable to stay healthy, so he was unable to reinforce the starting rotation, and it's tough to pencil him in for 2020 either.

The fallout from the team's trashcan-banging and other acts of hubris more properly falls under 2020 outlook, below. —*Matthew Trueblood*

Prospect Outlook

The Astros started the year with a significant amount of high-end talent in the upper levels with thinning, but still strong, depth in the middle to lower levels. But throughout the year the ranks were ravaged by promotions, some strange injuries, and a big trade. Yordan Alvarez had a massive campaign in Triple-A before finally getting promoted and running through major-league pitching like a hot knife through butter. Additional debuts included Cionel Pérez, Urquidy, Garrett Stubbs, Abraham Toro, and Bryan Abreu. One expected promotion that never came was that of **Forrest Whitley**, who struggled with injuries and inconsistencies. He seemingly came around at mid-season and gave a solid performance in the Arizona Fall League; he again looks like the potential top-of-the-rotation arm that had flashed five above average-or-better offerings, albeit with fringy command. And, of course, the Astros sent a crew including Martin and two strange profiles in Seth Beer and J.B. Bukauskas to the Diamondbacks in the Greinke trade.

What remains are some interesting profile arms that have predictably advanced feel for spinning breaking balls and a group of hitters with impressive plate discipline and spin recognition. Pitchers **Tyler Ivey** and **Cristian Javier** both had something akin to breakout seasons, their above-average fastballs and impressive pitch mixes overpowering Double-A hitters despite their questionable command. **Brandon Bielak** continued to look like a future No. 6 starter with impressive feel for a plus curveball and average command, but with fringy fastball velocity and an average changeup. **Freudis Nova** played half a season in Low-A as a 19-year-old but must transition his loud offensive tools to actual production. Catcher **Korey Lee** was drafted by the Astros in the first round and was above average in short-season ball.

This system has simply been picked through and ended the 2019 season considerably weaker than it had been at the beginning. Ultimately, though, the farm director and development crew deserve a pat on the back. They both fostered talent that helped them come within a game of winning the World Series and produced players that were traded for one of the premier arms in all of baseball. This is exactly what a World Series team should look to do with its farm system; this is also what you'd expect it to look like after they'd done it. There are some nice pieces left—Whitley still stands on top—so the Astros will still get help from the system down the road. They will need to build up the depth and high-end talent again before their system can rebound. The draft picks lost to their sign-stealing activities will, obviously, not help. —*Kevin Carter*

2020 Outlook

Houston's winter was defined by several hundred bangs and a few whimpers. The team made half-hearted noises about bringing back some of its departing free agents, and there were rumors that they would try to make a major addition behind the plate, but nothing much came of either. As controversy swirled and the team lost its chief baseball decision-maker, they froze up and failed to supplement a roster that needs something. At this writing, the only gesture towards making up for the departures of Cole, Miley, Héctor Rondón, Collin McHugh and Chirinos, was to sign a backup catcher and a fringy reliever or two, adding Dustin Garneau and Austin Pruitt. Their biggest acquisition of the winter, albeit one made desperately necessary when A.J. Hinch was suspended and then fired, was Dusty Baker…and actually, that's not so bad. Baker gets another chance to finally win a World Series as a skipper, and the Astros get the big heart, the old-school tenacity, and the tangible connection to the history

of the game that they'd been missing for a decade. Any gesture on the part of this franchise towards humanity rather than soulless efficiency is welcome.
—Matthew Trueblood

Performance Graphs

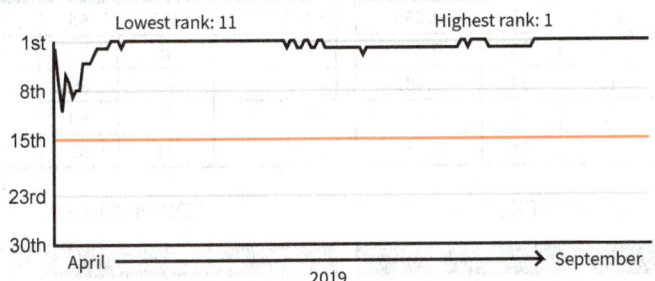

2019 Hit List Ranking

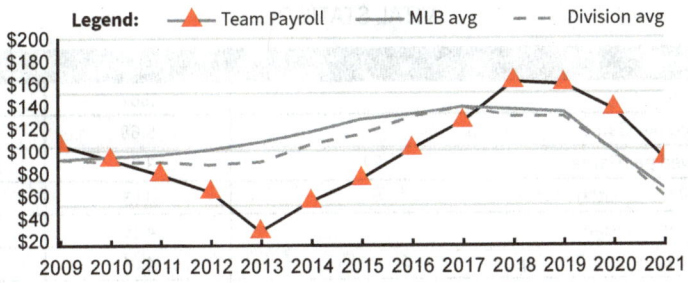

Committed Payroll (in millions)

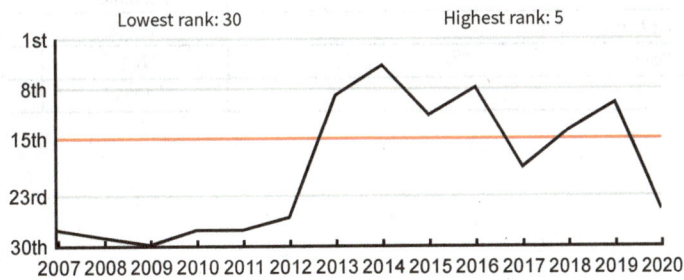

Farm System Ranking

2019 Team Performance

ACTUAL STANDINGS

Team	W	L	Pct
HOU	107	55	0.660
OAK	97	65	0.599
TEX	78	84	0.481
LAA	72	90	0.444
SEA	68	94	0.420

THIRD-ORDER STANDINGS

Team	W	L	Pct
HOU	117	45	0.719
OAK	95	67	0.584
LAA	73	89	0.453
SEA	72	90	0.444
TEX	71	91	0.437

TOP HITTERS

Player	WARP
Alex Bregman	8.6
George Springer	5.4
Yuli Gurriel	3.4

TOP PITCHERS

Player	WARP
Justin Verlander	7.9
Gerrit Cole	7.9
Ryan Pressly	1.6

VITAL STATISTICS

Statistic Name	Value	Rank
Pythagenpat	.667	2nd
Runs Scored per Game	5.68	3rd
Runs Allowed per Game	3.95	2nd
Deserved Runs Created Plus	115	1st
Deserved Run Average	4.10	3rd
Fielding Independent Pitching	4.01	3rd
Defensive Efficiency Rating	.729	1st
Batter Age	29.0	28th
Pitcher Age	30.1	27th
Salary	$158.0M	9th
Marginal $ per Marginal Win	$2.5M	25th
Injured List Days	701	2nd
$ on IL	12%	7th

2020 Team Projections

PROJECTED STANDINGS

Team	W	L	Pct	+/-
HOU	98.3	63.7	0.607	-9
LAA	86.8	75.2	0.536	15
OAK	84.6	77.4	0.522	-12
TEX	73.0	89.0	0.451	-5
SEA	66.0	96.0	0.407	-2

TOP PROJECTED HITTERS

Player	WARP
Alex Bregman	6.2
George Springer	4.9
Yordan Alvarez	4.0

TOP PROJECTED PITCHERS

Player	WARP
Justin Verlander	4.8
Zack Greinke	3.1
Jose Urquidy	1.8

FARM SYSTEM REPORT

Top Prospect	Number of Top 101 Prospects
Forrest Whitley, #26	3

KEY DEDUCTIONS

Player	WARP
Gerrit Cole	5.3
Héctor Rondón	0.7
Wade Miley	0.7
Will Harris	0.7
Robinson Chirinos	0.1
Jake Marisnick	-0.2

KEY ADDITIONS

Player	WARP
Taylor Jones	0.9
Cristian Javier	0.4
Enoli Paredes	0.4
Austin Pruitt	0.4
Jared Hughes	0.1
Nivaldo Rodriguez	0.1
Blake Taylor	0.0
Dustin Garneau	-0.1
Kent Emanuel	-0.3

Team Personnel

General Manager
James Click

Assistant GM, Player Development
Pete Putila

Special Assistant, Player Personnel
Kevin Goldstein

Senior Director, Baseball Strategy
Bill Firkus

Manager
Dusty Baker

BP Alumni
James Click
Kevin Goldstein
Ryan Lind

Minute Maid Park Stats

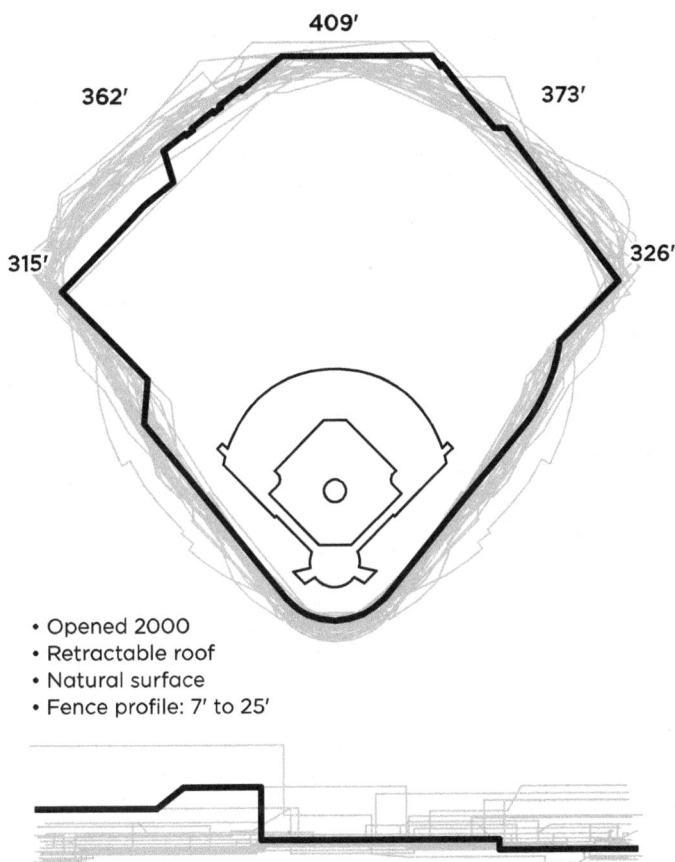

- Opened 2000
- Retractable roof
- Natural surface
- Fence profile: 7' to 25'

Three-Year Park Factors

Runs	Runs/RH	Runs/LH	HR/RH	HR/LH
99	99	99	106	103

Astros Team Analysis

All 30 of the team essays in this book are, by definition, failures. I say this in part, of course, to abnegate responsibility for my own personal failure on these pages, but also because it's true. Each author is trying to impose order on utter randomness, which is futile.

This is a normal human impulse. Consciousness—even the limbic-cortex-level sort—depends on this. Look at those trees: Is there a threat lurking? Is there one of those Pleistocene-era megafauna sloths hiding behind that dumpster? Why didn't A.J. Hinch go to Gerrit Cole in the 7th inning of Game 7 of the World Series?

The idea that our existence is nothing more than a series of random events and has no meaning is too terrifying to contemplate, and so we set about distracting ourselves. We mate and raise children, we watch sports, we go to work; we expend terrific amounts of energy to add structure to our lives. We are meaning-making beings.

"Moneyball," to the extent that term still has any meaning, is rooted in the same impulse. Front offices do their best to reduce variance; they stack marginal improvement on marginal improvement to increase their odds of winning. The "best" teams develop new metrics to quantify the previously unquantifiable in an effort to wring every iota of certitude from the available data. What started as a scrappy, under-resourced team looking for an edge has developed into a bloodless business of consultants willing to win at virtually any cost. Call it the McKinsey-fication of baseball.

The Astros, headed by ex-McKinsey consultant Jeff Luhnow, have proven better at this than most. Luhnow has proven willing to make marginal moves that other GMs aren't, from overseeing a genuine tanking effort early in his tenure to risking PR disaster by acquiring distressed assets (see Osuna, Roberto). Despite missing on a No. 1 overall pick or two, Luhnow has overseen a remarkable transformation of the Astros, shepherding them through their transition to the AL to a World Series win in 2017 and another appearance this past year.

But even Luhnow's level of ISO 9001-level scientifically derived certitude wasn't enough. In 2017, the Astros players set out to determine what would happen before it happened. They melded high tech with low to relay the signs of the opposing battery to hitters by using cameras in the stands and a trash can in the clubhouse. This scheme appears to have worked remarkably well before it was exposed. What we know about the sign-stealing scheme maps pretty well to a substantial drop in team strikeouts in 2017, and may have continued through 2019, when they boat raced the AL West and finished the season with the best record in baseball.

We're still processing what we know about the Astros' cheating; new information is coming to light, and Major League Baseball has not yet leveled any penalties on the team, players, or staff. But it very well may be that cameras and trash cans will be the legacy of the 2019 Astros.

One imagines Brandon Taubman was thrilled when the Astros' cheating efforts came to light. This new scandal blew his scandal completely out of the news cycle. But for a minute there, after the Astros lost the World Series but before allegations of cheating became the focus, some Houston fans were compelled to blame him for the loss. After all, following the Taubman incident, the Astros dropped games 1 and 2 of the World Series at home, where they were all but unbeatable. Then, they mitigated in the most mild of terms the PR disaster they created by proffering a marginally satisfactory apology about Taubman's repugnant behavior, and won the next three games. How could this be anything other than karmic retribution?

Well, because it's just not, that's how. Shit doesn't work like that. That's the meaning-making impulse at its worst and most misleading.

The Astros didn't lose because Brandon Taubman did something awful or because the Astros picked up Roberto Osuna as a distressed asset. (Osuna's poor pitching in the World Series absolutely was a factor, however.) The way this game (and this society) is structured, front offices have perverse incentives to acquire people like Osuna; this is baseball under late capitalism, our national pastime in the early 21st century. As long as the PR blowback is less detrimental than the cost-savings is beneficial, teams will sign perpetrators of domestic violence. (We can have a discussion about the concept of punishment and forgiveness elsewhere, but I'll remind you that Osuna faced no real legal punishment for his actions; the charges against him were dropped when Osuna agreed to submit to the equivalent of a restraining order and undergo counseling. He also, of course, received a 75-game suspension and was sent packing by the Blue Jays, which is how we got here.)

No, the Astros lost the World Series because the Nationals beat them in seven weird and hard-fought games. Before the World Series, though, the Astros were golden gods.

When the regular season ended on September 29, 2019, the Astros had the best record in baseball and were the prohibitive favorites to win the World Series. The Astros had:

- The AL Cy Young winner and runner-up
- The probable AL MVP runner-up
- The AL Rookie of the Year

- The best record in baseball
- The best home record in baseball and home-field advantage throughout the playoffs

and still managed to lose to the Nationals (an extremely good team, despite the narrative some writers have overlaid onto their weird and circuitous journey to a World Series championship, but on paper not nearly the generationally good club the Astros were).

So why look at 180 random events—in this case, baseball games—and attempt to craft a narrative? Some of us hope that a postmortem of the season will help us understand what went well, what went poorly, and how this might inform what happens in 2020. Or perhaps you don't follow this club closely, and you're looking to these pages for an abstract, a summary, a story. See chaos; impose order. Normal human impulse.

A 107-win season was the result of a painstaking rebuild orchestrated primarily by Jeff Luhnow. Luhnow was retained as GM in 2011 and the Astros moved from the NL Central to the AL West in 2013. They lost 111 games that year and secured yet another number one draft pick—their third in three years—which Luhnow spent on Carlos Correa. Mark Appel and Brady Aiken were also drafted during Luhnow's tenure, which serves to remind us that number-one picks are anything but a lock.

Luhnow and staff hit paydirt with Alex Bregman in 2015, whom the Astros were able to select because they failed to sign Aiken the previous year. All Bregman did last year was mount an MVP campaign that logged him 8.6 BWARP, second only to some guy who patrols the outfield in Anaheim. Houston also picked Kyle Tucker at no. 5 overall that year, who did much better last season than in his 2018 call-up. Tucker showed glimpses of what his future could be, with the kind of stringy power that, if you squint, looks something like Cody Bellinger's. But Tucker's contributions would likely be getting a lot more adulation if it weren't for another 22-year-old rookie who's made an even bigger splash.

Yordan Alvarez, whom Houston got from the Dodgers for Josh Fields in 2016, has been a revelation. He made his debut in early June and appeared in 87 games and quickly amassed 2.8 WARP. He looked overmatched in the DS and CS playoff rounds, but found his footing again in the World Series against the Nationals, hitting a bomb to help his team win Game 5 and showing a veteran eye at the plate, spitting on pitches from some of the most devious hurlers in the game. He was the Astros' first rookie of the year to win the award unanimously.

Most fanbases would jump at the chance to have either a legit starter or a ROY power-hitting corner infielder emerge from their minor-league chain in a single season; in Alvarez and Jose Urquidy, the Astros had both.

Houston Astros 2020

Urquidy came out of nowhere, starting the season at Double-A Corpus Christi and ending up taking the ball to start game 4 of the World Series. The 24-year-old's pitch mix, command and control, and unflappableness on the mound means he'll likely slide into the rotation in 2020.

The Astros system is so deep, in fact, that they weathered IL stints by some of their superstars—George Springer and José Altuve missed 31 and 39 days, respectively, and Correa was out for 87—and they still won 107 games. Of course, it helps when you have Bregman to slide over to shortstop when your All-Star starter goes down. Eight pitchers also spent time on the IL, notably Lance McCullers and Collin McHugh. None of this is 2019 Yankees-level injury-bug stuff, but not every org can paper over these kinds of losses, much less fill those gaps and post the best record in baseball.

In fact, it's probably only possible if instead of a starting rotation you have a Cerberus comprising three of the greatest pitchers in the game. The Astros let Dallas Keuchel walk and filled the void with an unholy amalgamation of guys like Framber Valdez and Corbin Martin, plus a third of a season of Zack Greinke.

Adding Greinke to a rotation that already included a resurgent Justin Verlander and a peak Gerrit Cole seemed borderline unfair. Cole inked a record-setting deal to suit up for the Yankees, today, tomorrow, and forever, but Greinke and Verlander will still be in blue and orange for the next two years. Add a healthy Brad Peacock, the aforementioned Urquidy, and a fifth starter TBD—Valdez, or, dare to dream, a functional Forrest Whitley?—and the Astros rotation looks as fearsome as any in baseball though 2021.

The only obvious hole is at catcher. Martín Maldonado and Robinson Chirinos were adequate behind the dish last season in their walk years. Maldonaldo returns on a two-year deal, but Chirinos departs as a free agent. With Yasmani Grandal off the board early, the pickins were slim. But the Astros are nothing if not resourceful.

The Astros likely could've made a run at Grandal. Had they made a competitive offer, one assumes he would've jumped at the chance to play in Houston, handle an elite pitching staff, and play half his games in the shadow of the Crawford Boxes. The only thing that stopped them from signing Grandal (or re-signing Cole, for that matter) is money. But it's not just the salaries and the competitive balance surtax we're talking about here. There's also the…see, this is difficult to talk about, because we all know it's happening, but no one is quite sure what to call it. Let's try, instead of a capital strike, a capital slowdown. The competitive balance tax functionally acts as a salary cap, giving cover to any owner inclined to plead poverty. And even as team profits and valuations have exploded, the CBT hasn't remotely kept pace. Since 2009, the average franchise's value has increased 300 percent; during that same time, the CBT has increased 27 percent.

According to Forbes, the average MLB team is worth $1.78B, and no team is worth less than a billion dollars. The Marlins could have, at the dawn of 2019 free agency, gone out and signed Rendon, Cole, and Grandal and they'd still be worth a billion dollars. Hell, they might be worth *more* considering people might even buy tickets to see that team. There were no objective financial factors stopping your favorite team from signing Gerrit Cole; the austerity is coming from inside the ownership group. This is why we'll almost certainly have a "work stoppage" in 2021, when the current collective bargaining agreement expires. The first-year player draft, the arbitration process, and free agency (especially compensation picks) all function to depress player salaries. What kinds of concessions the Players Association under Tony Clark will be able to extract from ownership remains to be seen. What, if anything, will a union called the *Major* League Baseball Players Association do to address the staggering exploitation occurring throughout the minor leagues?

Ultimately no one knows what will happen in 2020 or beyond. Hell, we don't really even know what happened in 2019. There's no objective truth anywhere, but especially not here. All we have are the narratives we've constructed, replete with our blind spots, biases, and misinterpretations. Give typewriters to an infinite number of baseball fans and ask them to craft a narrative about the Astros season, and you'd get an infinite number of different responses, each one trying to make meaning where no such thing exists. Or, as I like to call it, the internet.

—Ian Miller is half of Productive Outs and a quarter of Puig Destroyer.

Part 2: Player Analysis

Houston Astros 2020

PLAYER COMMENTS WITH GRAPHS

José Altuve 2B
Born: 05/06/90   Age: 30   Bats: R   Throws: R
Height: 5'6"   Weight: 165   Origin: International Free Agent, 2007

YEAR	TEAM	LVL	AGE	PA	R	2B	3B	HR	RBI	BB	K	SB	CS	AVG/OBP/SLG
2017	HOU	MLB	27	662	112	39	4	24	81	58	84	32	6	.346/.410/.547
2018	HOU	MLB	28	599	84	29	2	13	61	55	79	17	4	.316/.386/.451
2019	HOU	MLB	29	548	89	27	3	31	74	41	82	6	5	.298/.353/.550
2020	HOU	MLB	30	595	77	28	2	25	83	44	91	21	7	.292/.351/.490

Comparables: Rennie Stennett, Alexi Casilla, Rod Carew

Good Financial Cents dot com says the best way to invest $10,000 is to play it safe and put it in a High Yielding Savings Account. Baseball Prospectus dot com encourages you to simply give it to an undersized, but scrappy child who will one day become a superstar. Still hampered by a knee issue sustained halfway through 2018, Altuve looked decidedly not himself to start last season. There were whispers in Houston that perhaps the Astros would regret the 7-year, $163.5 million extension inked with him. When he went to the IL in early May, he was hitting .243. Turns out having a healthy knee is one of the things required to succeed at the big-league level, because Altuve finished the season slashing .320/.363/.581. One of the easiest people in the game to root for, Altuve remains an elite talent.

YEAR	TEAM	LVL	AGE	PA	DRC+	VORP	BABIP	BRR	FRAA	WARP
2017	HOU	MLB	27	662	140	65.0	.370	2.7	2B(149): -0.1	5.6
2018	HOU	MLB	28	599	126	41.4	.352	2.4	2B(130): -7.9	3.2
2019	HOU	MLB	29	548	119	31.8	.303	-0.5	2B(121): -0.6, SS(1): 0.0	3.0
2020	HOU	MLB	30	595	119	38.2	.312	0.6	2B -4	3.5

José Altuve, continued

Batted Ball Distribution

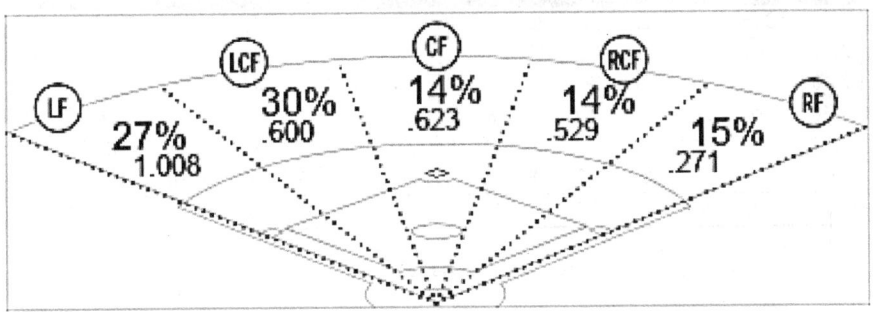

Strike Zone vs LHP **Strike Zone vs RHP**

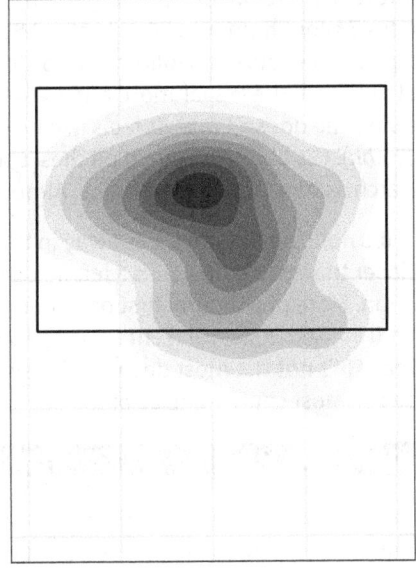

Yordan Alvarez OF/1B

Born: 06/27/97   Age: 23   Bats: L   Throws: R
Height: 6'5"   Weight: 225   Origin: International Free Agent, 2016

YEAR	TEAM	LVL	AGE	PA	R	2B	3B	HR	RBI	BB	K	SB	CS	AVG/OBP/SLG
2017	QUD	A	20	139	26	6	0	9	33	23	36	2	0	.360/.468/.658
2017	BCA	A+	20	252	19	11	3	3	36	19	41	6	1	.277/.329/.393
2018	CCH	AA	21	190	39	13	0	12	46	19	45	5	2	.325/.389/.615
2018	FRE	AAA	21	189	24	8	0	8	28	23	47	1	0	.259/.349/.452
2019	ROU	AAA	22	253	50	16	0	23	71	38	50	2	1	.343/.443/.742
2019	HOU	MLB	22	369	58	26	0	27	78	52	94	0	0	.313/.412/.655
2020	HOU	MLB	23	595	93	28	1	42	108	70	151	4	1	.279/.367/.576

Comparables: Austin Riley, Austin Meadows, Clint Frazier

Conveying how terrifying Alvarez is at the plate is simultaneously a laughably simple and incredibly complex task. His frame fills the entire batter's box and he moves with a silence that borders on imposing. A mere lift of his bat portends future harm to an innocent baseball. On the one hand, it's a text, no subtext. He hits 474-foot homers. He's a Michael Bay movie at the plate, complete with the necessary explosions followed by a slow-motion trot around the bases. On the other hand, there's far more nuance. Much like jazz, Alvarez's success is in the swings he doesn't take. It feels like he knows what pitch is coming (*Editor's note: Uhhhh*). His ability to lay off pitches just outside the zone is almost as fun to watch as him launching dingers. Almost.

It's not true that he takes away in the field what he brings to the plate, but it is closer than you'd like. He's a left fielder in the same way that going to the dentist is fun. More of a natural first baseman, he's not going to displace Yuli Gurriel until at least 2021. He'll enter his age-23 season as a unanimous Rookie of the Year. He's not the most decorated player in the Astros lineup, but he might just be the most captivating at-bat.

YEAR	TEAM	LVL	AGE	PA	DRC+	VORP	BABIP	BRR	FRAA	WARP
2017	QUD	A	20	139	190	18.1	.449	-1.6	LF(13): -1.5, 1B(7): 0.0	1.3
2017	BCA	A+	20	252	117	6.6	.316	-0.2	LF(28): 2.6, 1B(15): -0.4	1.1
2018	CCH	AA	21	190	172	21.5	.377	0.2	LF(31): 3.6, 1B(5): -0.1	2.1
2018	FRE	AAA	21	189	110	5.3	.315	-2.0	LF(34): -6.3	-0.2
2019	ROU	AAA	22	253	176	36.1	.355	-2.3	LF(27): 0.3, 1B(9): -1.1	2.4
2019	HOU	MLB	22	369	149	29.9	.366	-0.5	LF(10): -0.5	2.8
2020	HOU	MLB	23	595	140	38.9	.314	-0.4	LF: -1	3.9

Yordan Alvarez, continued

Batted Ball Distribution

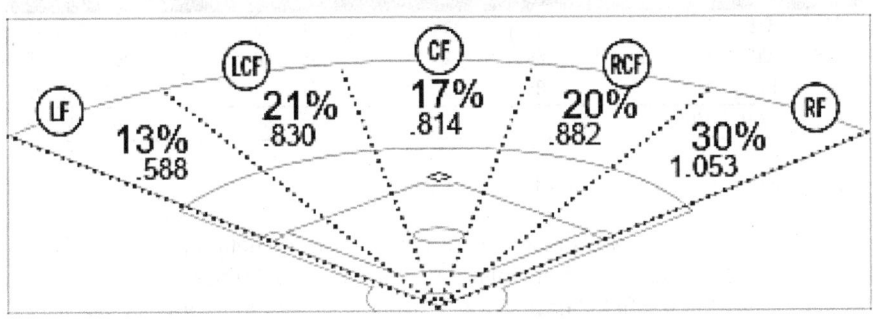

Strike Zone vs LHP   Strike Zone vs RHP

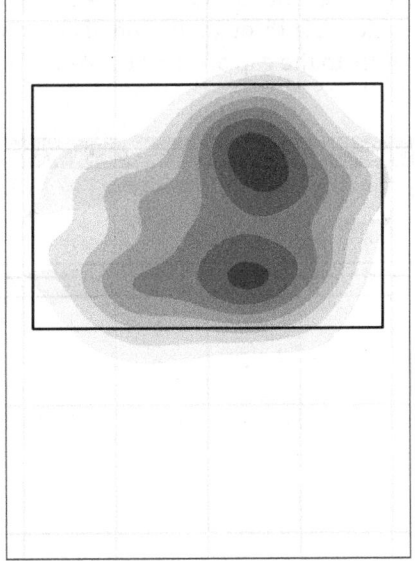

Michael Brantley LF

Born: 05/15/87   Age: 33   Bats: L   Throws: L
Height: 6'2"   Weight: 200   Origin: Round 7, 2005 Draft (#205 overall)

YEAR	TEAM	LVL	AGE	PA	R	2B	3B	HR	RBI	BB	K	SB	CS	AVG/OBP/SLG
2017	CLE	MLB	30	375	47	20	1	9	52	31	50	11	1	.299/.357/.444
2018	CLE	MLB	31	631	89	36	2	17	76	48	60	12	3	.309/.364/.468
2019	HOU	MLB	32	637	88	40	2	22	90	51	66	3	2	.311/.372/.503
2020	HOU	MLB	33	560	66	29	1	19	71	47	65	11	3	.283/.349/.456

Comparables: Johnny Damon, Darin Erstad, Melky Cabrera

"Uncle Mike" was a steady presence both on and off the field for an Astros team that saw many of its best hitters miss time with injuries. Suffice it to stay "steady" and "on the field" haven't been used together often for Brantley, which is probably why Cleveland failed to dispense a qualifying offer following 2018. Defying the odds, Brantley put together a second straight season of over 140 games played, improving his walk rate and ISO in the process. He has the skill set to turn into a Launch Angle Guy and add some power as he continues to thicken out through the end of his prime, but he seems content to lash line drives to the gap and ring up 35-40 doubles per year. It's not a bad gig if you can get it.

YEAR	TEAM	LVL	AGE	PA	DRC+	VORP	BABIP	BRR	FRAA	WARP
2017	CLE	MLB	30	375	106	14.5	.325	-0.6	LF(87): 5.2	1.7
2018	CLE	MLB	31	631	118	31.3	.319	1.4	LF(134): -3.4	2.8
2019	HOU	MLB	32	637	122	34.1	.320	0.0	LF(120): -7.4, RF(9): -0.8	2.5
2020	HOU	MLB	33	560	112	23.1	.295	-0.1	LF -3	2.1

Michael Brantley, continued

Batted Ball Distribution

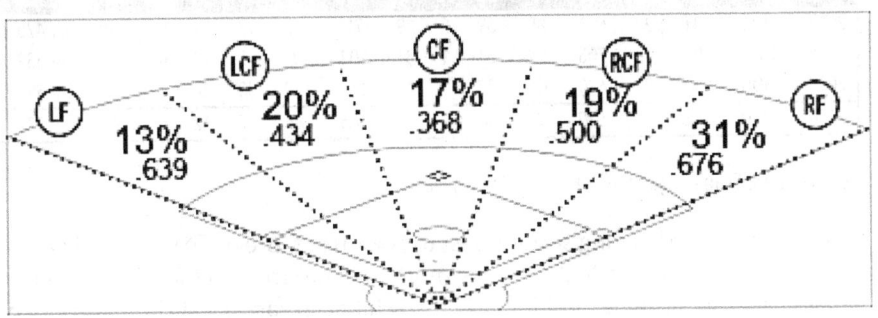

Strike Zone vs LHP   **Strike Zone vs RHP**

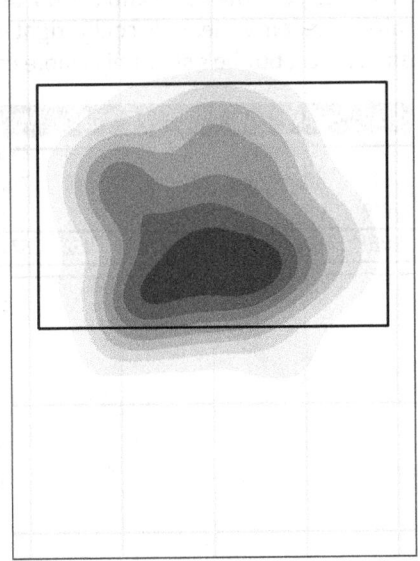

Alex Bregman 3B

Born: 03/30/94 Age: 26 Bats: R Throws: R
Height: 6'0" Weight: 180 Origin: Round 1, 2015 Draft (#2 overall)

YEAR	TEAM	LVL	AGE	PA	R	2B	3B	HR	RBI	BB	K	SB	CS	AVG/OBP/SLG
2017	HOU	MLB	23	626	88	39	5	19	71	55	97	17	5	.284/.352/.475
2018	HOU	MLB	24	705	105	51	1	31	103	96	85	10	4	.286/.394/.532
2019	HOU	MLB	25	690	122	37	2	41	112	119	83	5	1	.296/.423/.592
2020	HOU	MLB	26	630	97	36	2	36	106	92	87	12	5	.292/.404/.572

Comparables: Evan Longoria, Bob Horner, Jim Ray Hart

There's no shame in being second-best to Mike Trout. Bregman was nothing short of phenomenal in 2019, walking more than he struck out for the second straight season, flashing additional value by filling in capably at shortstop when he wasn't manning third base. He overcame a slow start to the season (five homers through May 1st) to come a few votes away from giving the Astros a clean sweep in the major award voting. For whatever being the Face of Baseball means to both the sport and the player, Bregman seems ready and willing to take on that mantle. He's cocky, right up to, and sometimes past, the point of annoyance, but he's spent his whole career backing it up.

YEAR	TEAM	LVL	AGE	PA	DRC+	VORP	BABIP	BRR	FRAA	WARP
2017	HOU	MLB	23	626	114	35.5	.311	-1.5	3B(132): 8.7, SS(30): -2.9	3.9
2018	HOU	MLB	24	705	150	71.7	.289	-1.6	3B(136): 5.4, SS(28): -0.4	7.4
2019	HOU	MLB	25	690	157	80.6	.281	-3.8	3B(99): 6.6, SS(65): 4.7	8.6
2020	HOU	MLB	26	630	152	57.7	.292	-2.2	3B 5, SS 0	6.6

Alex Bregman, continued

Batted Ball Distribution

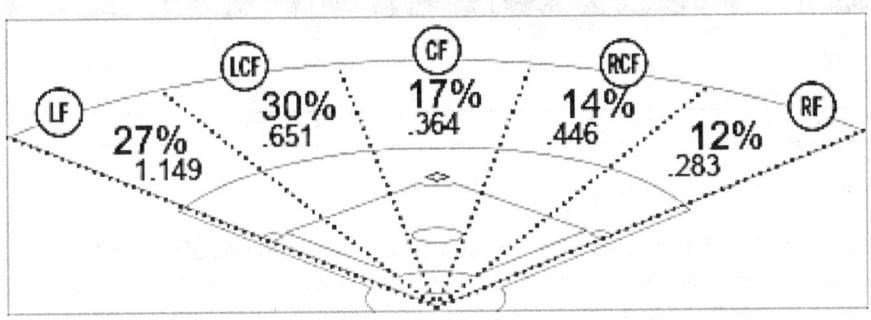

Strike Zone vs LHP   **Strike Zone vs RHP**

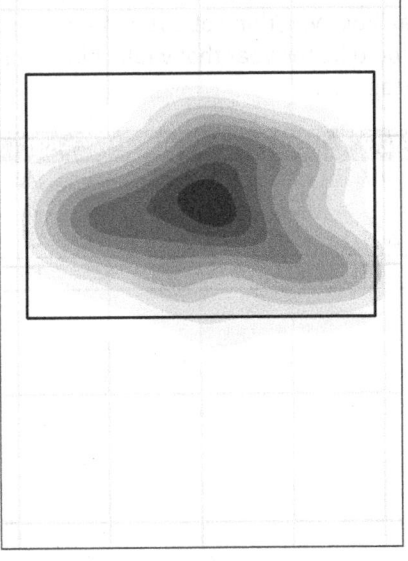

Houston Astros 2020

Carlos Correa SS

Born: 09/22/94   Age: 25   Bats: R   Throws: R
Height: 6'4"   Weight: 215   Origin: Round 1, 2012 Draft (#1 overall)

YEAR	TEAM	LVL	AGE	PA	R	2B	3B	HR	RBI	BB	K	SB	CS	AVG/OBP/SLG
2017	HOU	MLB	22	481	82	25	1	24	84	53	92	2	1	.315/.391/.550
2018	HOU	MLB	23	468	60	20	1	15	65	53	111	3	0	.239/.323/.405
2019	HOU	MLB	24	321	42	16	1	21	59	35	75	1	0	.279/.358/.568
2020	HOU	MLB	25	525	72	24	1	28	81	56	122	9	3	.266/.349/.503

Comparables: Corey Seager, Rougned Odor, Freddie Freeman

Since his debut in 2015 as a 20-year-old, Correa has been one of the best shortstops in baseball. A string of injuries have limited his time on the field, but there is no arguing that when he's healthy, Correa is a generational talent. He leads all shortstops in DRC+ during his career with a healthy gap between him and Francisco Lindor in second place (123 to 117). His arm belongs in the museum at the NASA Space Center alongside all of Houston's other famous rockets, and his 6-foot-4 frame allows him to make up for whatever he lacks in agility. Everything about him screams superstardom and every year feels like it could be the year that vaults him firmly into the upper echelon of major-leaguers.

YEAR	TEAM	LVL	AGE	PA	DRC+	VORP	BABIP	BRR	FRAA	WARP
2017	HOU	MLB	22	481	140	48.2	.352	-3.0	SS(108): -1.4	4.1
2018	HOU	MLB	23	468	98	20.4	.282	0.8	SS(109): 7.2	2.8
2019	HOU	MLB	24	321	126	26.5	.303	-0.6	SS(75): -2.3	2.3
2020	HOU	MLB	25	525	122	33.7	.303	-1.0	SS 1	3.6

Carlos Correa, continued

Batted Ball Distribution

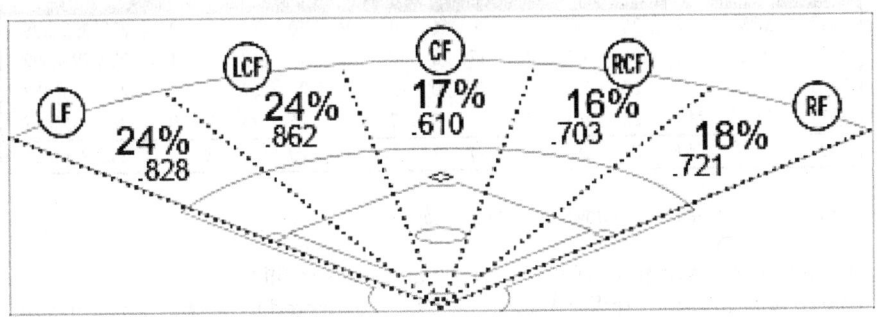

Strike Zone vs LHP   **Strike Zone vs RHP**

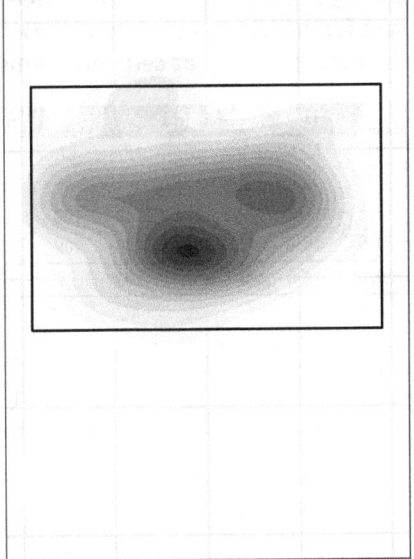

Aledmys Díaz INF

Born: 08/01/90   Age: 29   Bats: R   Throws: R
Height: 6'1"   Weight: 195   Origin: International Free Agent, 2014

YEAR	TEAM	LVL	AGE	PA	R	2B	3B	HR	RBI	BB	K	SB	CS	AVG/OBP/SLG
2017	MEM	AAA	26	187	19	9	1	4	26	10	30	3	3	.253/.305/.388
2017	SLN	MLB	26	301	31	17	0	7	20	13	42	4	1	.259/.290/.392
2018	TOR	MLB	27	452	55	26	0	18	55	23	62	3	4	.263/.303/.453
2019	HOU	MLB	28	247	36	12	1	9	40	26	28	2	0	.271/.356/.467
2020	HOU	MLB	29	280	32	14	1	10	35	20	44	3	2	.252/.316/.433

Comparables: Stephen Drew, Jordy Mercer, Johnny Logan

When the Astros acquired Díaz, it was clear he was to fill the Marwin González role of plug-and-play utility man who was not expected to dazzle or disappoint. Through the end of May, he filled that role admirably, playing in 60 percent of Houston's games at six different positions. Unfortunately, hamstring and foot injuries limited him to 69 games. All in all, though, he looked comfortable serving as a human Swiss Army Knife. With Yordan Alvarez locking up the DH spot for the foreseeable future, the Astros will need to find other ways to spell their starters and Díaz certainly seems capable of doing just that.

YEAR	TEAM	LVL	AGE	PA	DRC+	VORP	BABIP	BRR	FRAA	WARP
2017	MEM	AAA	26	187	77	4.9	.281	-1.2	SS(28): 2.3, 3B(9): -0.6	0.5
2017	SLN	MLB	26	301	80	2.4	.282	-1.3	SS(68): -10.6, 3B(4): -0.2	-0.6
2018	TOR	MLB	27	452	108	18.9	.269	-1.8	SS(95): -5.8, 3B(38): -0.5	1.5
2019	HOU	MLB	28	247	109	10.1	.268	1.9	1B(26): -0.8, 2B(25): 0.6	1.1
2020	HOU	MLB	29	280	95	6.6	.269	-0.3	2B 1, 3B -1	0.5

Aledmys Díaz, continued

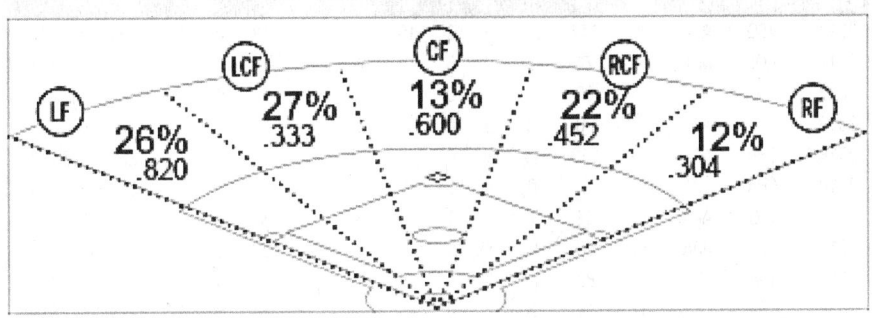

Strike Zone vs LHP   **Strike Zone vs RHP**

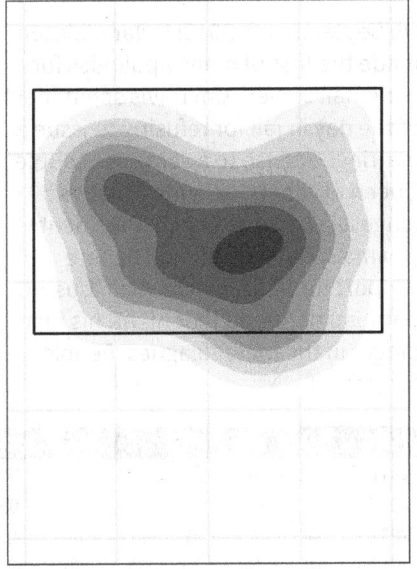

Dustin Garneau C

Born: 08/13/87   Age: 32   Bats: R   Throws: R
Height: 6'2"   Weight: 205   Origin: Round 19, 2009 Draft (#571 overall)

YEAR	TEAM	LVL	AGE	PA	R	2B	3B	HR	RBI	BB	K	SB	CS	AVG/OBP/SLG
2017	ABQ	AAA	29	144	24	9	2	10	26	13	22	0	1	.281/.347/.617
2017	COL	MLB	29	74	5	7	0	1	6	4	24	0	0	.206/.260/.353
2017	OAK	MLB	29	52	5	1	0	1	3	8	12	0	0	.159/.288/.250
2018	NAS	AAA	30	80	8	3	0	2	9	5	10	0	0	.208/.263/.333
2018	CHR	AAA	30	160	19	9	0	7	22	16	38	0	2	.252/.340/.468
2018	CHA	MLB	30	3	0	0	0	0	1	1	0	0	0	.500/.667/.500
2019	LVG	AAA	31	32	2	2	1	1	3	3	9	0	0	.308/.387/.577
2019	SLC	AAA	31	98	16	8	0	6	13	11	28	0	0	.229/.347/.542
2019	LAA	MLB	31	82	11	3	0	2	7	8	18	0	0	.232/.346/.362
2019	OAK	MLB	31	19	3	2	0	1	7	2	4	0	0	.294/.368/.588
2020	HOU	MLB	32	210	24	9	0	10	28	18	58	1	0	.214/.296/.420

Comparables: Ron Karkovice, Chris Herrmann, Tim Spehr

On September 9, 2015, Hillary Clinton made the first of many apologies for her email server. Kim Davis spent most of the day in jail for refusing to issue a marriage license to a same sex couple. Queen Elizabeth became Britain's longest serving monarch. President Obama sought additional Senate support for his Iran deal. Also, Dustin Garneau homered that night, his first dinger in the major leagues. People forget that.

YEAR	TEAM	P. COUNT	FRM RUNS	BLK RUNS	THRW RUNS	TOT RUNS
2017	ABQ	5165	-3.2	0.2	0.7	-2.7
2017	COL	2719	-1.3	-1.0	0.0	-2.6
2017	OAK	2146	-1.0	-0.6	0.3	-1.5
2018	CHA	154	0.0	0.1	0.0	1.5
2018	NAS	2347	-2.1	-0.2	0.7	-0.9
2018	CHR	5299	0.0	0.0	0.4	1.3
2019	LAA	3366	0.4	0.0	0.0	0.4
2019	SLC	3832	7.2	0.1	0.6	7.7
2019	OAK	690	0.1	-0.2	0.0	0.4
2020	HOU	9423	-5.8	-0.2	0.1	-5.8

YEAR	TEAM	LVL	AGE	PA	DRC+	VORP	BABIP	BRR	FRAA	WARP
2017	ABQ	AAA	29	144	124	14.7	.265	0.2	C(36): -1.9	1.0
2017	COL	MLB	29	74	68	0.9	.302	0.8	C(22): -0.1	0.1
2017	OAK	MLB	29	52	69	-0.9	.194	-0.3	C(18): 0.0	0.0
2018	NAS	AAA	30	80	70	-2.1	.210	-1.3	C(18): -2.2	-0.3
2018	CHR	AAA	30	160	118	8.8	.295	-0.3	C(39): -0.9, LF(1): -0.2	0.8
2018	CHA	MLB	30	3	98	0.7	.500	0.0	C(1): -0.3	0.0
2019	LVG	AAA	31	32	99	1.6	.412	-1.0	C(7): -0.1, 1B(1): 0.0	0.1
2019	SLC	AAA	31	98	91	3.7	.265	-0.6	C(26): 8.7	1.1
2019	LAA	MLB	31	82	88	2.9	.286	-0.5		0.2
2019	OAK	MLB	31	19	109	1.2	.333	-0.2	C(7): 0.0	0.1
2020	HOU	MLB	32	210	87	6.3	.253	0.0	C -6	0.0

Dustin Garneau, *continued*

Batted Ball Distribution

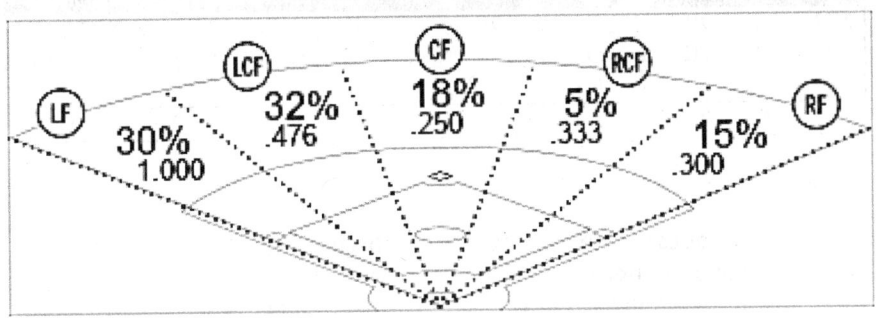

Strike Zone vs LHP **Strike Zone vs RHP**

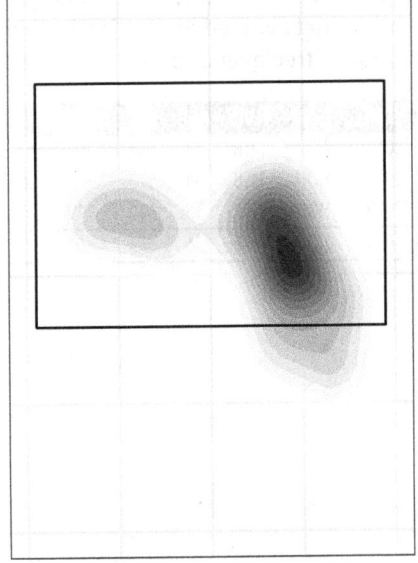

Yuli Gurriel CI

Born: 06/09/84 Age: 36 Bats: R Throws: R
Height: 6'0" Weight: 190 Origin: International Free Agent, 2016

YEAR	TEAM	LVL	AGE	PA	R	2B	3B	HR	RBI	BB	K	SB	CS	AVG/OBP/SLG
2017	HOU	MLB	33	564	69	43	1	18	75	22	62	3	2	.299/.332/.486
2018	HOU	MLB	34	573	70	33	1	13	85	23	63	5	1	.291/.323/.428
2019	HOU	MLB	35	612	85	40	2	31	104	37	65	5	3	.298/.343/.541
2020	HOU	MLB	36	595	69	33	1	25	82	28	75	4	2	.274/.315/.469

Comparables: Ray Knight, Bill Madlock, Charlie Hayes

The way he torques his arms and twists all of his body weight to his front foot is wholly unique to Gurriel. Nothing about his approach seems like it should work. He swings at everything. His 37 walks were by far a career-best and it just feels like there should not be any power in his bat, but from the middle of July to the end of the season, he sustained an OPS above 1.000. And he is a very good defender at first base to boot, specifically when it comes to backhanded picks that he perfected early in his career as a third baseman. In November, the Astros and Gurriel avoided arbitration by inking a $8.3 million contract giving him the option of free agency at the end of the 2020 season.

YEAR	TEAM	LVL	AGE	PA	DRC+	VORP	BABIP	BRR	FRAA	WARP
2017	HOU	MLB	33	564	109	18.6	.308	-1.7	1B(131): 8.4, 3B(7): -0.3	2.1
2018	HOU	MLB	34	573	109	20.3	.306	1.1	1B(109): 1.5, 3B(21): 1.2	2.0
2019	HOU	MLB	35	612	119	29.0	.289	-1.5	1B(110): 7.3, 3B(42): 0.4	3.4
2020	HOU	MLB	36	595	102	12.5	.280	-0.6	1B 9	2.2

Yuli Gurriel, continued

Batted Ball Distribution

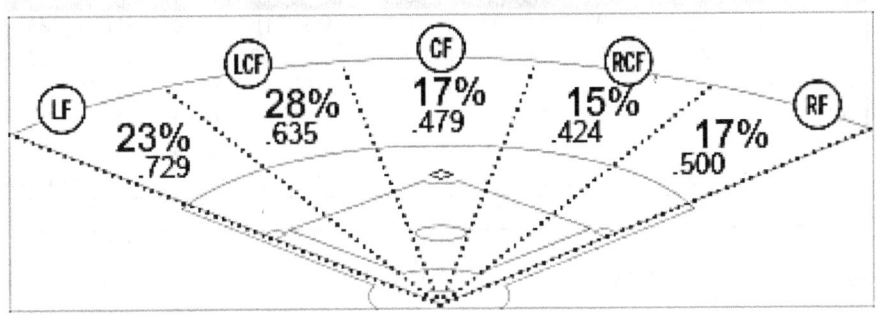

Strike Zone vs LHP   **Strike Zone vs RHP**

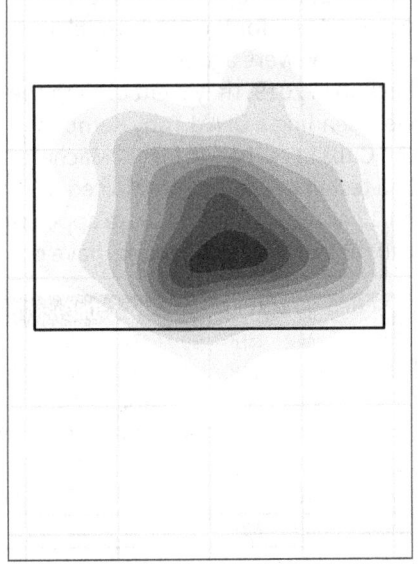

Houston Astros 2020

Martín Maldonado C

Born: 08/16/86 Age: 33 Bats: R Throws: R
Height: 6'0" Weight: 230 Origin: Round 27, 2004 Draft (#803 overall)

YEAR	TEAM	LVL	AGE	PA	R	2B	3B	HR	RBI	BB	K	SB	CS	AVG/OBP/SLG
2017	LAA	MLB	30	471	43	19	1	14	38	15	119	0	2	.221/.276/.368
2018	LAA	MLB	31	290	24	14	0	5	32	13	73	0	1	.223/.284/.332
2018	HOU	MLB	31	114	15	4	1	4	12	3	25	0	0	.231/.257/.398
2019	KCA	MLB	32	263	26	15	0	6	17	17	55	0	0	.227/.291/.366
2019	CHN	MLB	32	13	0	0	0	0	0	2	5	0	0	.000/.154/.000
2019	HOU	MLB	32	98	20	4	0	6	10	13	26	0	0	.202/.316/.464
2020	HOU	MLB	33	350	35	13	0	11	38	27	89	1	1	.205/.282/.353

Comparables: Miguel Montero, Welington Castillo, Jeff Mathis

It's like the old saying goes: If you love someone, let them go ... and just trade for them again next year. Maldonado left in free agency after the Astros acquired him for the 2018 stretch run. When they were again in need of a backup in 2019, they went back to the well, sending a DFA'd Tony Kemp to the Cubs in exchange for "El Machete."

YEAR	TEAM	P. COUNT	FRM RUNS	BLK RUNS	THRW RUNS	TOT RUNS
2017	LAA	18609	27.2	1.0	3.2	32.0
2018	LAA	11256	4.1	-0.8	0.3	4.0
2018	HOU	4686	1.7	-0.3	0.2	2.5
2019	KCA	10448	-1.4	3.3	0.3	2.1
2019	CHN	571	-0.1	-0.3	0.0	0.1
2019	HOU	3404	-0.5	0.9	-0.3	0.6
2020	HOU	15936	3.1	1.0	0.2	4.3

In a testament to just how juiced the 2019 baseball was, Maldonado somehow hit 12 home runs in 374 plate appearances. An owner of a 36 percent career caught stealing rate, runners have poorly donated outs to Maldonado.

YEAR	TEAM	LVL	AGE	PA	DRC+	VORP	BABIP	BRR	FRAA	WARP
2017	LAA	MLB	30	471	73	2.2	.273	-2.4	C(137): 32.1, 1B(1): 0.0	3.8
2018	LAA	MLB	31	290	74	3.1	.287	-0.1		0.6
2018	HOU	MLB	31	114	75	-0.3	.263	-0.6	C(40): 2.0	0.4
2019	KCA	MLB	32	263	76	5.9	.270	-4.6	C(73): 1.8	0.3
2019	CHN	MLB	32	13	-25	-1.5	.000	-0.1	C(4): -0.2	-0.2
2019	HOU	MLB	32	98	97	4.6	.212	0.0	C(26): 0.1, 1B(1): 0.0	0.5
2020	HOU	MLB	33	350	67	-0.2	.249	-1.5	C 4	0.4

Martín Maldonado, continued

Batted Ball Distribution

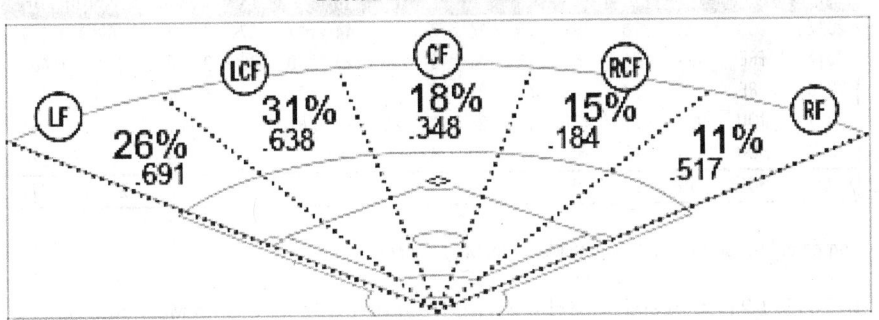

Strike Zone vs LHP   **Strike Zone vs RHP**

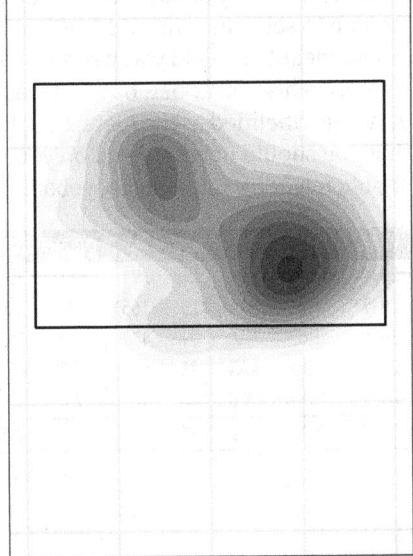

Jack Mayfield MI

Born: 09/30/90 Age: 29 Bats: R Throws: R
Height: 5'11" Weight: 190 Origin: Undrafted Free Agent, 2013

YEAR	TEAM	LVL	AGE	PA	R	2B	3B	HR	RBI	BB	K	SB	CS	AVG/OBP/SLG
2017	CCH	AA	26	291	39	16	2	14	44	17	57	7	2	.289/.330/.519
2017	FRE	AAA	26	165	28	12	0	6	23	10	30	3	0	.273/.321/.468
2018	FRE	AAA	27	479	66	31	1	16	66	33	92	5	4	.270/.324/.457
2019	ROU	AAA	28	431	78	26	1	26	79	37	78	7	1	.287/.350/.566
2019	HOU	MLB	28	65	8	5	0	2	5	1	16	0	0	.156/.169/.328
2020	HOU	MLB	29	35	4	2	0	2	5	2	9	0	0	.232/.285/.444

Comparables: Tommy Field, Tommy Manzella, Mike Yastrzemski

In 2013, 1,216 players were chosen in the June draft, including Mark Appel at No. 1 overall by the Astros. Mayfield was not one of them. He finished his senior season at Oklahoma with a .711 OPS and the Astros signed him, undoubtedly with the assumption that he would help round out a lineup card in the lower levels of the minors. But then he started hitting. And hitting. And suddenly you look up to see him with a .916 OPS at Triple-A. Injuries to essentially the entire infield meant Mayfield was needed in the majors. He hit a double off Cole Hamels in his first at-bat, but that was the highlight of a season where he looked very overwhelmed at the plate. Still, he played in the big leagues and proved that you should never give up on your dreams, and more importantly, you should never try to predict baseball.

YEAR	TEAM	LVL	AGE	PA	DRC+	VORP	BABIP	BRR	FRAA	WARP
2017	CCH	AA	26	291	121	22.0	.317	1.3	2B(43): -1.8, SS(20): 0.9	1.6
2017	FRE	AAA	26	165	95	8.0	.305	2.1	3B(17): 2.5, 2B(14): -1.6	0.7
2018	FRE	AAA	27	479	110	21.1	.304	-0.2	2B(62): -6.3, SS(48): -8.9	0.7
2019	ROU	AAA	28	431	118	41.7	.291	0.0	SS(42): -1.5, 2B(33): 2.9	2.5
2019	HOU	MLB	28	65	73	0.7	.174	-0.6	SS(21): 0.2, 2B(5): -0.2	0.0
2020	HOU	MLB	29	35	87	0.8	.262	0.0	2B 0	0.0

Jack Mayfield, continued

Batted Ball Distribution

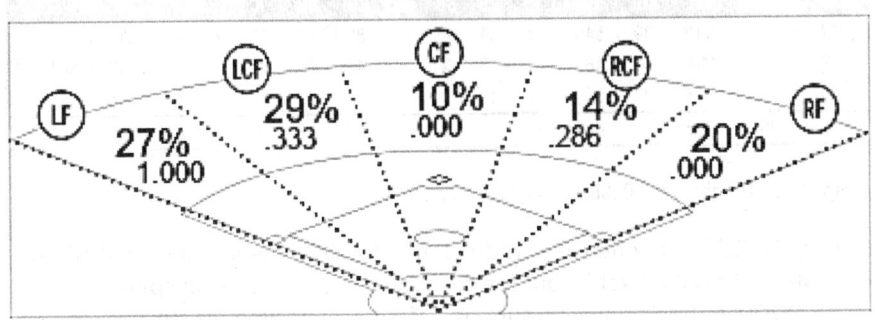

Strike Zone vs LHP   **Strike Zone vs RHP**

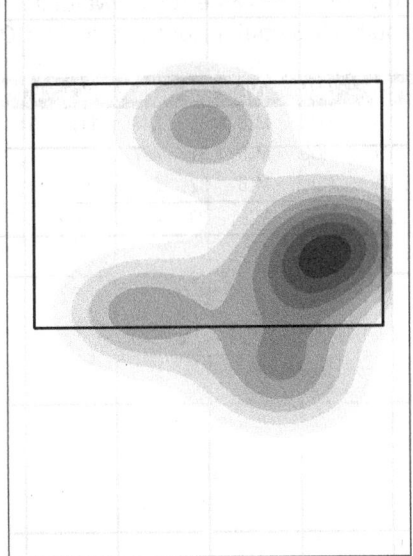

Houston Astros 2020

Josh Reddick RF

Born: 02/19/87   Age: 33   Bats: L   Throws: R
Height: 6'2"   Weight: 195   Origin: Round 17, 2006 Draft (#523 overall)

YEAR	TEAM	LVL	AGE	PA	R	2B	3B	HR	RBI	BB	K	SB	CS	AVG/OBP/SLG
2017	HOU	MLB	30	540	77	34	4	13	82	43	72	7	3	.314/.363/.484
2018	HOU	MLB	31	487	63	13	2	17	47	49	77	7	2	.242/.318/.400
2019	HOU	MLB	32	550	57	19	3	14	56	36	66	5	2	.275/.319/.409
2020	HOU	MLB	33	420	46	17	2	14	51	32	60	6	2	.265/.323/.424

Comparables: Dwight Evans, Bubba Trammell, Trot Nixon

WOOOOOO Reddick's offensive production *WOOOOOO* has started to fall off. You hope *WOOOOOO* it is fixable, but the dip in power and loss of bat speed *WOOOOOOO* is almost always a sure sign of a guy in decline. He still has the *WOOOOOOOOO* defensive prowess to rob some dingers from Minute Maid *WOOOOOO* Park's short right field fence and can make any third base coach sweat with his arm *WOOOOOOOO* so there's definitely still value there. However, *WOOOOOO* with Kyle Tucker waiting in the wings, Houston may let that value (and his $13 million contract) find *WOOOOOO* a home elsewhere.

YEAR	TEAM	LVL	AGE	PA	DRC+	VORP	BABIP	BRR	FRAA	WARP
2017	HOU	MLB	30	540	119	34.1	.339	2.5	RF(102): -1.6, LF(48): -1.2	2.4
2018	HOU	MLB	31	487	106	10.3	.258	-1.0	RF(111): -2.0, LF(43): 0.4	1.2
2019	HOU	MLB	32	550	97	11.6	.288	-2.2	RF(119): 5.2, LF(29): -1.1	1.3
2020	HOU	MLB	33	420	97	7.7	.284	-0.2	RF 0, CF 0	0.7

Josh Reddick, continued

Batted Ball Distribution

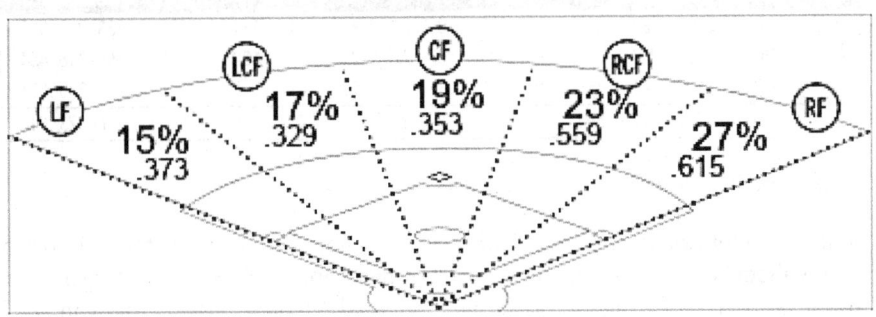

Strike Zone vs LHP **Strike Zone vs RHP**

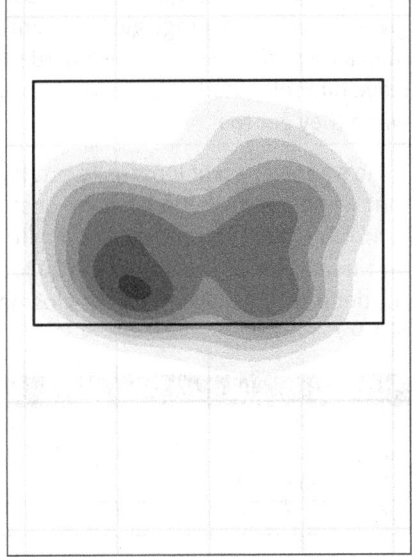

Houston Astros 2020

George Springer CF

Born: 09/19/89 Age: 30 Bats: R Throws: R
Height: 6'3" Weight: 215 Origin: Round 1, 2011 Draft (#11 overall)

YEAR	TEAM	LVL	AGE	PA	R	2B	3B	HR	RBI	BB	K	SB	CS	AVG/OBP/SLG
2017	HOU	MLB	27	629	112	29	0	34	85	64	111	5	7	.283/.367/.522
2018	HOU	MLB	28	620	102	26	0	22	71	64	122	6	4	.265/.346/.434
2019	HOU	MLB	29	556	96	20	3	39	96	67	113	6	2	.292/.383/.591
2020	HOU	MLB	30	595	90	22	1	37	100	70	129	9	5	.278/.373/.540

Comparables: Tim Salmon, Mike Young, Jay Bruce

A beloved clubhouse presence, Springer finally harnessed his raw talent into the MVP-caliber season of which he always seemed capable. Despite missing a month with a hamstring injury, Springer finished 7th on a loaded American League ballot. One of the game's most dangerous leadoff hitters, he set a franchise record with 10 leadoff home runs in 2019 and now has 36 in his young career, putting him well within striking distance of franchise legend Craig Biggio's National League record of 53. He's not as fast as you would think he is given his above-average glove in center field [he finished outside the top 100 in Statcast's sprint speed leaderboard in 2019]. At some point even that speed will leave him relegated to the corner outfield, but the Astros will cross that bridge when they get to it.

He's gone to great lengths to put together competitive at-bats, something that was a real struggle when he posted a 33 percent strikeout rate in his rookie year. Time flies when you're having fun and somehow Springer is already set to be a free agent at the end of the 2020 season unless an extension is agreed to. His departure would signal the closing of no doubt the greatest chapter in Astros history.

YEAR	TEAM	LVL	AGE	PA	DRC+	VORP	BABIP	BRR	FRAA	WARP
2017	HOU	MLB	27	629	130	41.6	.297	0.5	CF(84): 2.6, RF(78): 0.6	4.5
2018	HOU	MLB	28	620	114	30.1	.303	1.5	CF(80): -2.8, RF(77): 2.6	2.9
2019	HOU	MLB	29	556	141	46.6	.305	2.5	CF(75): 2.4, RF(59): 4.1	5.4
2020	HOU	MLB	30	595	136	48.9	.305	1.3	CF -1, RF 1	5.1

George Springer, continued

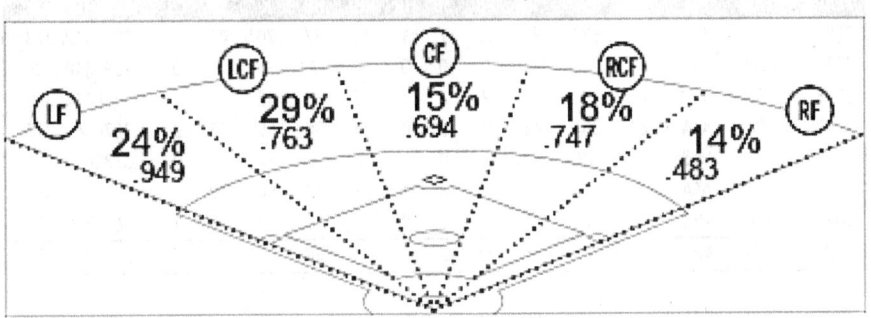

Strike Zone vs LHP   **Strike Zone vs RHP**

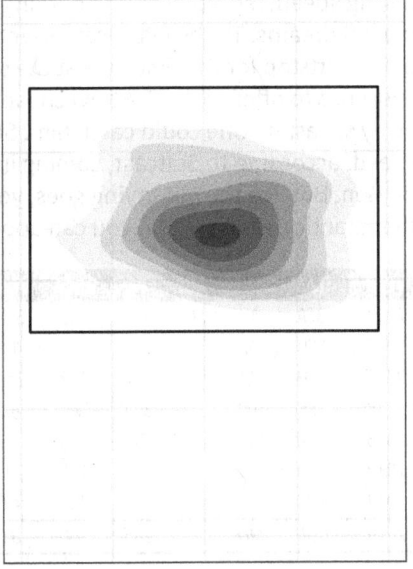

Myles Straw UT

Born: 10/17/94 Age: 25 Bats: R Throws: R
Height: 5'10" Weight: 180 Origin: Round 12, 2015 Draft (#349 overall)

YEAR	TEAM	LVL	AGE	PA	R	2B	3B	HR	RBI	BB	K	SB	CS	AVG/OBP/SLG
2017	BCA	A+	22	533	81	17	7	1	41	87	70	36	9	.295/.412/.373
2017	CCH	AA	22	54	9	0	0	0	3	7	9	2	0	.239/.340/.239
2018	CCH	AA	23	294	47	7	3	1	17	35	42	35	6	.327/.414/.390
2018	FRE	AAA	23	304	48	10	3	0	14	38	60	35	3	.257/.349/.317
2018	HOU	MLB	23	10	4	0	0	1	1	1	0	2	0	.333/.400/.667
2019	ROU	AAA	24	313	46	11	3	1	33	32	50	19	4	.321/.391/.394
2019	HOU	MLB	24	128	27	4	2	0	7	19	24	8	1	.269/.378/.343
2020	HOU	MLB	25	245	24	11	2	2	21	24	52	12	4	.274/.348/.366

Comparables: David Dellucci, Mallex Smith, Denard Span

A man stops you at a fork in the road and offers you two choices. Go right and you are destined to the life of a fifth-outfielder, forever doomed to be a light-hitting speedster representing nothing more than a pinch runner in your wildest playoff dreams. To the left is career-ending embarrassment as you attempt to play shortstop for the first time at the second-highest level of competition the sport has to offer. In 2019, Straw chose to punch that man in the face and run away so fast no one could catch him. Straw finished with a Top-5 average sprint speed, according to Statcast, coming in just behind Trea Turner and Byron Buxton. But like the old saying goes, you can't steal first base unless you're in the Atlantic League where you can apparently do whatever you want.

YEAR	TEAM	LVL	AGE	PA	DRC+	VORP	BABIP	BRR	FRAA	WARP
2017	BCA	A+	22	533	152	52.8	.347	5.5	CF(72): 6.9, RF(31): 7.2	6.6
2017	CCH	AA	22	54	92	1.8	.297	0.6	CF(11): -1.1, LF(2): 0.7	0.2
2018	CCH	AA	23	294	142	24.5	.386	4.4	CF(58): 6.0, RF(6): 2.0	3.4
2018	FRE	AAA	23	304	96	8.1	.330	3.8	CF(43): 4.9, RF(25): 1.4	1.8
2018	HOU	MLB	23	10	108	1.8	.250	0.7	RF(5): -0.1, CF(3): 0.0	0.1
2019	ROU	AAA	24	313	105	20.2	.386	2.5	CF(31): 4.9, SS(30): -1.1	1.9
2019	HOU	MLB	24	128	92	4.0	.345	3.5	SS(26): 1.4, CF(11): -0.8	0.8
2020	HOU	MLB	25	245	94	8.0	.350	0.8	CF 4, SS 0	1.3

Myles Straw, continued

Batted Ball Distribution

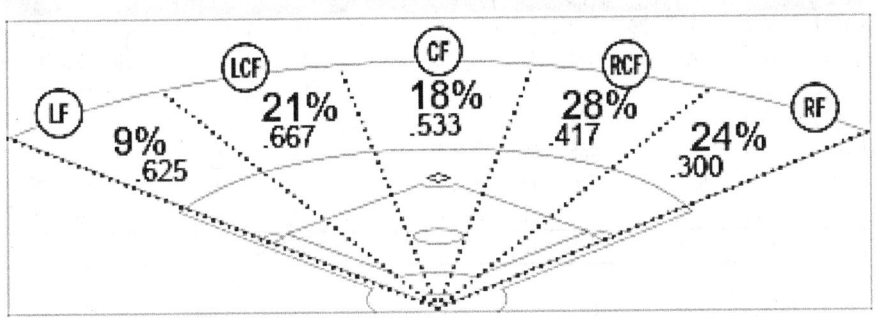

Strike Zone vs LHP

Strike Zone vs RHP

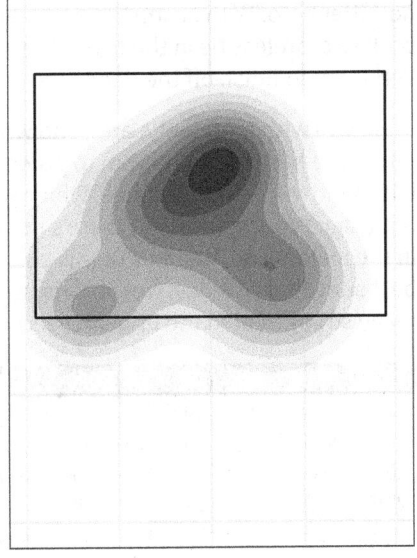

Abraham Toro 3B

Born: 12/20/96 Age: 23 Bats: B Throws: R
Height: 6'1" Weight: 190 Origin: Round 5, 2016 Draft (#157 overall)

YEAR	TEAM	LVL	AGE	PA	R	2B	3B	HR	RBI	BB	K	SB	CS	AVG/OBP/SLG
2017	TCV	A-	20	128	21	8	0	6	16	19	21	1	3	.292/.414/.538
2017	QUD	A	20	158	25	3	2	9	17	21	30	2	0	.209/.323/.463
2018	BCA	A+	21	349	54	20	1	14	56	45	62	5	1	.257/.361/.473
2018	CCH	AA	21	202	16	15	2	2	22	17	46	3	3	.230/.317/.371
2019	CCH	AA	22	435	65	22	4	16	70	48	77	4	1	.306/.393/.513
2019	ROU	AAA	22	79	17	9	0	1	10	10	5	0	1	.424/.506/.606
2019	HOU	MLB	22	89	13	3	2	2	9	9	19	1	1	.218/.303/.385
2020	HOU	MLB	23	105	12	4	1	4	14	9	23	0	0	.241/.314/.433

Comparables: Andy LaRoche, Dalton Pompey, Ryan Kalish

A multi-hyphenated player, this Venezuelan-Canadian former-catcher switch-hitter who now plays as many positions (first, second, and third) as languages spoken (English, Spanish and French) can add another hyphen to his resume: no-hitter hero. With Justin Verlander eight innings deep in a no-hitter, Toro broke a scoreless tie in the top of the ninth—in Toronto no less—to allow Verlander to finish off the deed.

He's 23 with a catcher's arm, and while he's still getting comfortable on the infield, he has the athleticism to potentially stick at the hot corner. Toro is a better hitter from the left side, which was even more apparent when he faced big-league southpaws. But there's no rush in Houston. The infield is set in stone in the majors and Aledmys Díaz is currently serving in the utility role Toro seems best suited for one day. Not surprisingly scouts are, uh, bullish on Toro after a really strong year in the upper levels of the minors.

YEAR	TEAM	LVL	AGE	PA	DRC+	VORP	BABIP	BRR	FRAA	WARP
2017	TCV	A-	20	128	190	14.2	.316	-2.1	3B(25): -2.5, C(6): -0.1	0.9
2017	QUD	A	20	158	113	11.2	.198	1.1	3B(17): 0.8, C(9): -0.2	0.9
2018	BCA	A+	21	349	156	31.2	.278	1.7	3B(81): 3.4	3.6
2018	CCH	AA	21	202	89	1.1	.298	-2.6	3B(43): -0.7	0.1
2019	CCH	AA	22	435	161	40.4	.346	-0.6	3B(85): 6.3, 2B(11): 0.2	4.6
2019	ROU	AAA	22	79	174	15.3	.443	1.9	3B(7): -0.7, 2B(4): -0.2	1.0
2019	HOU	MLB	22	89	79	1.0	.259	-0.1	3B(24): -0.8, 1B(1): 0.0	0.0
2020	HOU	MLB	23	105	95	1.8	.273	0.0	3B 1	0.3

Abraham Toro, continued

Batted Ball Distribution

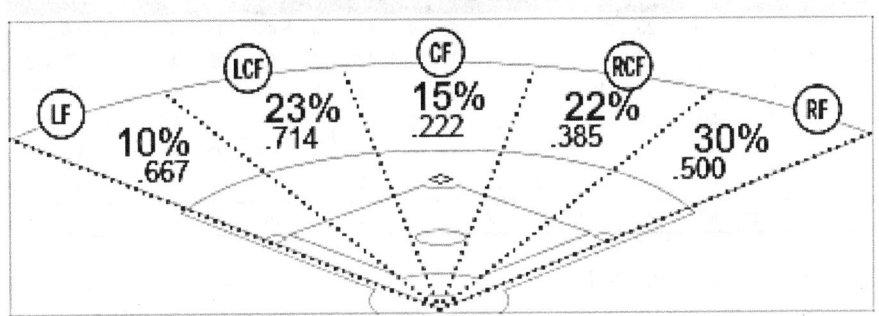

| Strike Zone vs LHP | Strike Zone vs RHP |

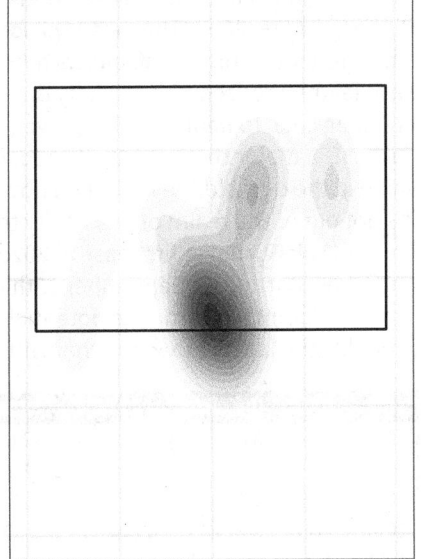

Kyle Tucker OF

Born: 01/17/97 Age: 23 Bats: L Throws: R
Height: 6'4" Weight: 190 Origin: Round 1, 2015 Draft (#5 overall)

YEAR	TEAM	LVL	AGE	PA	R	2B	3B	HR	RBI	BB	K	SB	CS	AVG/OBP/SLG
2017	BCA	A+	20	206	31	12	4	9	43	24	45	13	5	.288/.379/.554
2017	CCH	AA	20	318	39	21	1	16	47	22	64	8	4	.265/.325/.512
2018	FRE	AAA	21	465	86	27	3	24	93	48	84	20	4	.332/.400/.590
2018	HOU	MLB	21	72	10	2	1	0	4	6	13	1	1	.141/.236/.203
2019	ROU	AAA	22	536	92	26	3	34	97	60	116	30	5	.266/.354/.555
2019	HOU	MLB	22	72	15	6	0	4	11	4	20	5	0	.269/.319/.537
2020	HOU	MLB	23	420	54	19	2	24	64	32	104	11	4	.236/.302/.479

Comparables: Anthony Rizzo, Wil Myers, Victor Robles

One of the most important things for a batter to do is to make good contact. Tucker does that as well as anyone, sandwiching himself between J.D. Martinez and Freddie Freeman in Statcast's Barrels Per Plate Appearance. He finished tied for 24th in the league with unanimous Rookie of the Year Yordan Alvarez in Hard Hit Percentage (48.9). The next trick for Tucker to learn is to hit it where they ain't. His long, lanky frame allows him to crush pitches middle-out, but teams have learned to feed him a steady diet of elevated fastballs and back-foot breaking balls to neutralize his power. In what we're calling a Reverse Springer, Tucker is a major threat on the basepaths while providing next to no defensive value in the outfield. He has fallen down the defensive spectrum so much that it's not out of the realm of possibility that he and Yordan Alvarez will fight to back up Yuli Gurriel at first base in 2020. The Astros made Tucker a full-time outfielder starting on September 13th and he proceeded to slash .268/.333/.561 from that point forward. The potential for a breakout is there, but this is probably the last time we say that with confidence.

YEAR	TEAM	LVL	AGE	PA	DRC+	VORP	BABIP	BRR	FRAA	WARP
2017	BCA	A+	20	206	146	20.6	.336	-3.1	RF(19): -1.8, CF(17): 1.2	1.1
2017	CCH	AA	20	318	137	20.8	.286	1.2	CF(37): -5.3, RF(18): -1.4	1.4
2018	FRE	AAA	21	465	156	52.9	.364	1.7	RF(54): 0.3, LF(32): -0.4	4.3
2018	HOU	MLB	21	72	73	-5.7	.176	-0.4	LF(20): -2.1, RF(3): 0.2	-0.3
2019	ROU	AAA	22	536	114	36.6	.280	1.3	RF(60): 3.2, LF(39): -0.3	2.4
2019	HOU	MLB	22	72	87	0.6	.326	0.6	LF(11): -0.4, RF(11): 0.9	0.2
2020	HOU	MLB	23	420	98	8.8	.261	1.0	RF 1, LF -2	0.9

Kyle Tucker, continued

Batted Ball Distribution

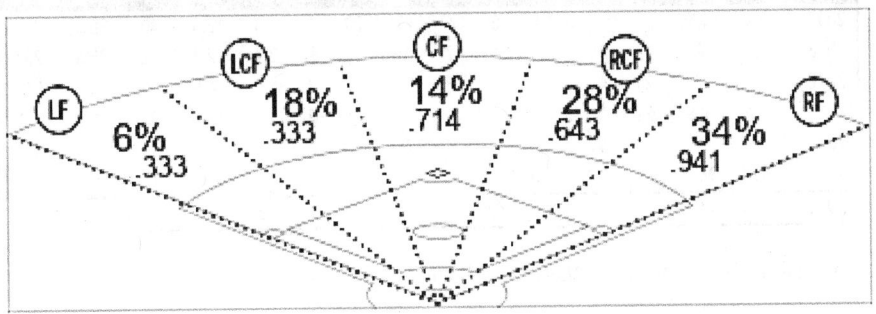

Strike Zone vs LHP   **Strike Zone vs RHP**

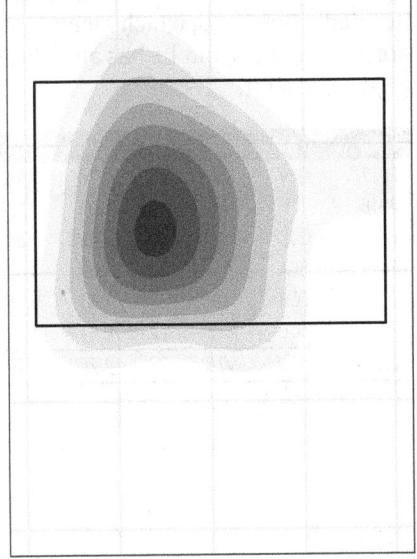

Bryan Abreu RHP

Born: 04/22/97 Age: 23 Bats: R Throws: R
Height: 6'1" Weight: 204 Origin: International Free Agent, 2013

YEAR	TEAM	LVL	AGE	W	L	SV	G	GS	IP	H	HR	BB/9	K/9	K	GB%	BABIP
2017	GRV	RK	20	1	3	0	8	6	29^1	29	4	6.4	12.3	40	38%	.357
2018	TCV	A-	21	2	0	0	4	2	16	11	2	3.4	12.4	22	35%	.281
2018	QUD	A	21	4	1	3	10	5	38^1	22	2	4.0	16.0	68	50%	.312
2019	BCA	A+	22	1	0	0	3	3	14^2	9	2	3.7	15.3	25	38%	.292
2019	CCH	AA	22	6	2	2	20	13	76^2	60	6	5.6	11.9	101	43%	.309
2019	HOU	MLB	22	0	0	0	7	0	8^2	4	0	3.1	13.5	13	50%	.250
2020	HOU	MLB	23	4	3	0	47	3	61	45	7	4.5	13.2	89	42%	.300

Comparables: Dylan Cease, Jorge Alcala, Victor Alcántara

Call him Jonah Hill because he skates on mid-90s stuff. Abreu left enough of an impression in 8 2/3 September innings to earn a spot on the ALCS roster. He has elite spin on both his slider and curveball and got whiffs on over half of swings against those pitches which is...hang on, calculating...good. The command is decidedly Not Good, which means any dreams of Abreu starting in the majors are gone for now, but he has already shown he can be successful in a very short big-league stint.

YEAR	TEAM	LVL	AGE	WHIP	ERA	DRA	WARP	MPH	FB%	WHF	CSP
2017	GRV	RK	20	1.70	7.98	5.52	0.2				
2018	TCV	A-	21	1.06	1.12	2.93	0.4				
2018	QUD	A	21	1.02	1.64	1.89	1.4				
2019	BCA	A+	22	1.02	3.68	3.09	0.3				
2019	CCH	AA	22	1.41	5.05	4.24	0.6				
2019	HOU	MLB	22	0.81	1.04	4.66	0.1	96.8	32.2	19.9	42.3
2020	HOU	MLB	23	1.25	3.49	3.49	1.2	96.7	33.3	20.6	43.8

Bryan Abreu, continued

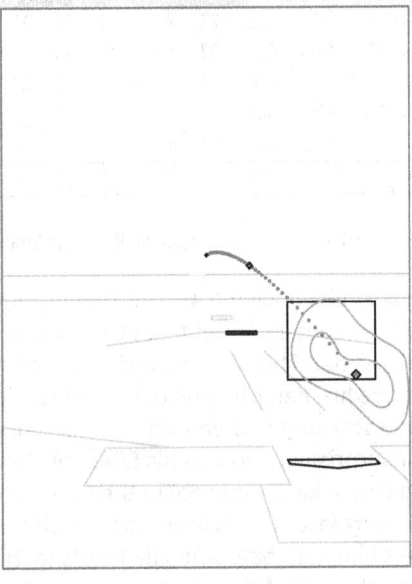

Type	Frequency	Velocity	H Movement	V Movement
● Fastball	32.2%	95.2 [108]	-6.5 [102]	-13.4 [107]
☐ Sinker				
+ Cutter				
▲ Changeup				
✕ Splitter				
▽ Slider				
◇ Curveball	65.1%	86.2 [125]	6.4 [96]	-41.4 [113]
⊕ Slow Curveball				
✱ Knuckleball				
▼ Screwball				

Rogelio Armenteros RHP

Born: 06/30/94 Age: 26 Bats: R Throws: R
Height: 6'1" Weight: 215 Origin: International Free Agent, 2014

YEAR	TEAM	LVL	AGE	W	L	SV	G	GS	IP	H	HR	BB/9	K/9	K	GB%	BABIP
2017	CCH	AA	23	2	3	1	14	10	65.1	49	3	2.6	10.2	74	42%	.284
2017	FRE	AAA	23	8	1	0	10	10	58.1	42	5	2.9	11.1	72	50%	.276
2018	FRE	AAA	24	8	1	1	22	21	118	106	15	3.7	10.2	134	38%	.301
2019	ROU	AAA	25	6	7	0	19	18	84.1	90	14	3.3	9.1	85	35%	.325
2019	HOU	MLB	25	1	1	1	5	2	18	17	1	2.5	9.0	18	38%	.314
2020	*HOU*	*MLB*	*26*	*5*	*4*	*0*	*32*	*10*	*70*	*68*	*13*	*3.5*	*8.1*	*63*	*36%*	*.280*

Comparables: Nick Tropeano, Aaron Blair, Dan Straily

It seems like having Arm 'n' Tear in your last name would be a bad sign for a pitcher, but all Armenteros has done since signing for $40,000 out of Cuba is get dudes out. This last one was a year of ups and downs for him. The Good: He made his major-league debut without looking overmatched. The Bad: His walk and strikeout and ground ball rates all were worse than in 2018, and unsurprisingly, so was his ERA. Still, he's big league ready and will have a chance to earn a back-end spot in the rotation come Spring Training. His low-90s sinking fastball lets him miss barrels with regularity and his changeup and curve lets him miss bats when he needs to. He throws them all in any location in any count (most of the times on purpose) and he evokes the energy of a wily 37-year-old veteran.

YEAR	TEAM	LVL	AGE	WHIP	ERA	DRA	WARP	MPH	FB%	WHF	CSP
2017	CCH	AA	23	1.04	1.93	3.08	1.6				
2017	FRE	AAA	23	1.05	2.16	2.24	2.2				
2018	FRE	AAA	24	1.31	3.74	3.97	2.1				
2019	ROU	AAA	25	1.43	4.80	4.61	1.7				
2019	HOU	MLB	25	1.22	4.00	5.23	0.1	94.3	48.4	11.7	43.2
2020	*HOU*	*MLB*	*26*	*1.36*	*4.80*	*4.72*	*0.6*	*93.9*	*49.2*	*11.9*	*44*

Rogelio Armenteros, continued

Pitch Shape vs LHH

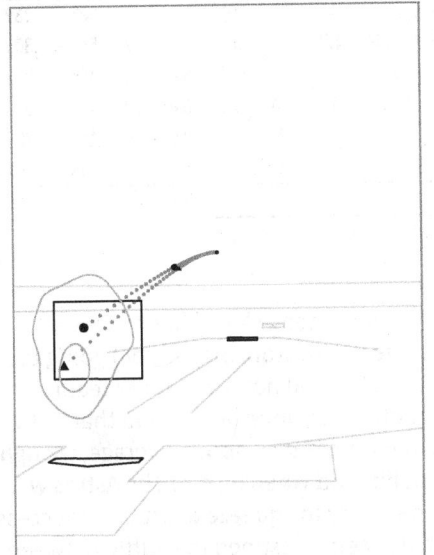

Pitch Shape vs RHH

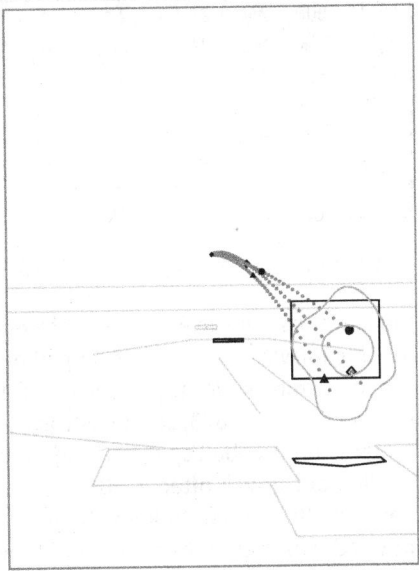

Type	Frequency	Velocity	H Movement	V Movement
● Fastball	48.3%	91.1 [96]	-3 [117]	-15.1 [102]
☐ Sinker				
+ Cutter				
▲ Changeup	28.5%	82.8 [91]	-11.3 [99]	-27.2 [101]
✕ Splitter				
▽ Slider	3.3%	84.6 [101]	5.3 [101]	-33.4 [99]
◇ Curveball	19.8%	78.9 [101]	8.2 [103]	-41 [114]
⊕ Slow Curveball				
✱ Knuckleball				
▼ Screwball				

Joe Biagini RHP

Born: 05/29/90 Age: 30 Bats: R Throws: R
Height: 6'5" Weight: 235 Origin: Round 26, 2011 Draft (#807 overall)

YEAR	TEAM	LVL	AGE	W	L	SV	G	GS	IP	H	HR	BB/9	K/9	K	GB%	BABIP
2017	BUF	AAA	27	1	1	0	4	4	17^1	13	2	3.1	7.3	14	58%	.239
2017	TOR	MLB	27	3	13	1	44	18	119^2	125	15	3.2	7.3	97	56%	.305
2018	BUF	AAA	28	0	3	0	4	4	21^2	19	1	3.3	5.4	13	45%	.257
2018	TOR	MLB	28	4	7	0	50	4	72	96	14	3.0	6.6	53	49%	.355
2019	TOR	MLB	29	3	1	1	50	0	50	50	8	3.1	9.0	50	45%	.309
2019	HOU	MLB	29	0	1	0	13	0	14^2	21	6	5.5	6.1	10	50%	.341
2020	HOU	MLB	30	2	2	0	44	0	47	47	7	3.5	7.8	40	49%	.299

Comparables: Burke Badenhop, Logan Ondrusek, Chris Leroux

Well, it turns out the Astros can't fix everybody. When asked what he was looking forward to upon learning of his trade to Houston, Biagini said going to space. He may have stayed earthside, but his ERA did not. He's under team control through 2023, so the Astros will continue to hope he can find that 2016 magic. His curveball spin rate and movement is still well above-average, though he did not throw it often in 2019 and it got hit hard when he did. The Astros will have an offseason to tinker with his arsenal to try to squeeze a last bit of success out of the former 28th-round pick. If not, he seems destined to shuttle between Triple-A and mop up duty in the big leagues.

YEAR	TEAM	LVL	AGE	WHIP	ERA	DRA	WARP	MPH	FB%	WHF	CSP
2017	BUF	AAA	27	1.10	3.12	3.50	0.4				
2017	TOR	MLB	27	1.40	5.34	3.98	2.0	95.9	52.9	9	47.1
2018	BUF	AAA	28	1.25	4.57	5.96	-0.1				
2018	TOR	MLB	28	1.67	6.00	5.72	-0.6	96.6	60.8	9.5	45.6
2019	TOR	MLB	29	1.34	3.78	4.73	0.3	95.5	48.5	14.3	43
2019	HOU	MLB	29	2.05	7.36	11.80	-1.0	95.0	48.5	9.3	42.9
2020	HOU	MLB	30	1.41	4.74	4.62	0.3	95.2	53.6	10.5	44.8

Joe Biagini, continued

Pitch Shape vs LHH	Pitch Shape vs RHH
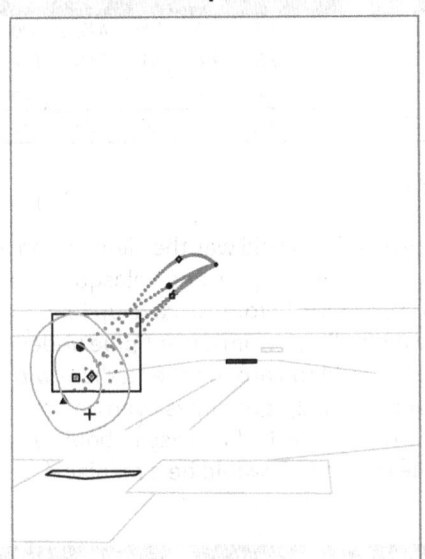	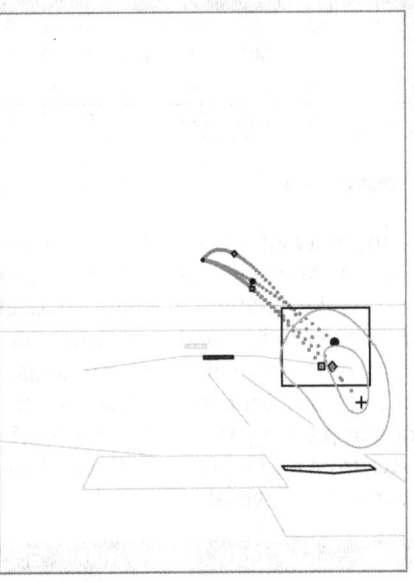

Type	Frequency	Velocity	H Movement	V Movement
● Fastball	16.8%	94 [105]	-3.3 [116]	-13 [108]
□ Sinker	34.0%	94.5 [110]	-9.9 [118]	-14.1 [122]
+ Cutter	29.6%	88.1 [96]	3.3 [109]	-27.6 [87]
▲ Changeup	10.8%	87.3 [108]	-10.3 [104]	-23.9 [110]
✕ Splitter				
▽ Slider				
◇ Curveball	8.7%	77.2 [95]	6.3 [95]	-57.6 [79]
⊕ Slow Curveball				
✱ Knuckleball				
▼ Screwball				

Chris Devenski RHP

Born: 11/13/90   Age: 29   Bats: R   Throws: R
Height: 6'3"   Weight: 210   Origin: Round 25, 2011 Draft (#771 overall)

YEAR	TEAM	LVL	AGE	W	L	SV	G	GS	IP	H	HR	BB/9	K/9	K	GB%	BABIP
2017	HOU	MLB	26	8	5	4	62	0	80^2	50	11	2.9	11.2	100	41%	.220
2018	HOU	MLB	27	2	3	2	50	1	47^1	42	9	2.5	9.7	51	37%	.275
2019	HOU	MLB	28	2	3	0	61	1	69	69	13	2.7	9.4	72	35%	.296
2020	HOU	MLB	29	3	3	0	55	0	58	51	9	2.9	10.2	66	35%	.286

Comparables: Fernando Salas, Derek Law, Huston Street

In the first half of the 2015 Texas League season, Devenski was the clear ace on a team that included names like McCullers, Hader, Feliz, Appel and Velasquez. He started the All-Star Game with a 1.16 ERA. Two starts before, he gave up four runs in six innings and got so mad that he did pull-ups from a giant pipe under the stadium until his arms were bruised. He would run around the stadium with one of those Bane masks that restrict your breathing, sometimes even on days he was pitching. He's a crazy person, is the point here. It's not easy to bounce back from a 5.49 DRA season, but if anyone can do it, it would be a maniacal worker like Devenski.

YEAR	TEAM	LVL	AGE	WHIP	ERA	DRA	WARP	MPH	FB%	WHF	CSP
2017	HOU	MLB	26	0.94	2.68	3.09	1.9	95.9	39.7	17.7	45.9
2018	HOU	MLB	27	1.16	4.18	3.61	0.7	96.2	41.6	15.2	46.7
2019	HOU	MLB	28	1.30	4.83	5.49	-0.1	96.7	44.1	13.7	46.6
2020	HOU	MLB	29	1.20	3.76	3.81	0.9	95.7	42.1	15.3	46.5

Chris Devenski, continued

Pitch Shape vs LHH

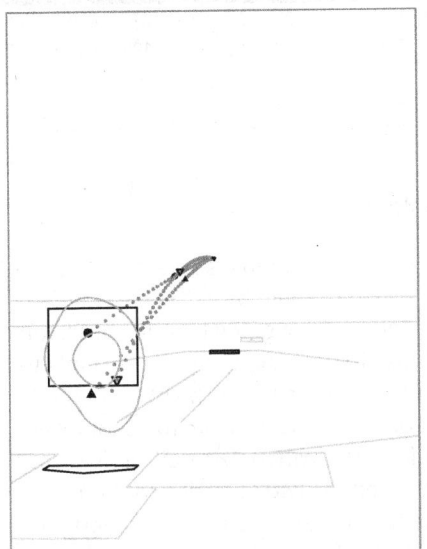

Pitch Shape vs RHH

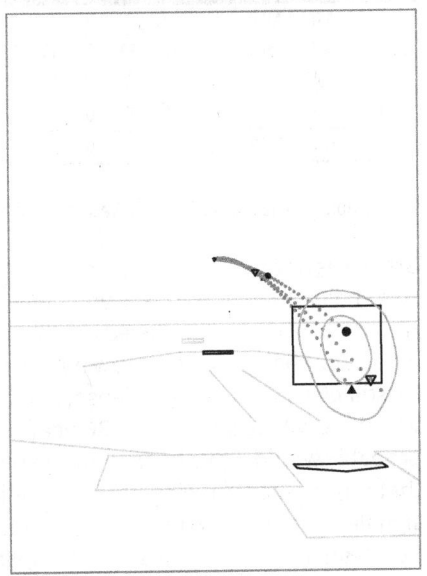

Type	Frequency	Velocity	H Movement	V Movement
● Fastball	44.1%	94.9 [107]	-9.2 [90]	-13.8 [106]
□ Sinker				
+ Cutter				
▲ Changeup	36.5%	84.2 [96]	-12.8 [92]	-31 [90]
✕ Splitter				
▽ Slider	19.4%	81.7 [89]	8.4 [114]	-36.3 [91]
◇ Curveball				
✥ Slow Curveball				
✴ Knuckleball				
▼ Screwball				

Zack Greinke RHP

Born: 10/21/83   Age: 36   Bats: R   Throws: R
Height: 6'2"   Weight: 200   Origin: Round 1, 2002 Draft (#6 overall)

YEAR	TEAM	LVL	AGE	W	L	SV	G	GS	IP	H	HR	BB/9	K/9	K	GB%	BABIP
2017	ARI	MLB	33	17	7	0	32	32	202^1	172	25	2.0	9.6	215	48%	.285
2018	ARI	MLB	34	15	11	0	33	33	207^2	181	28	1.9	8.6	199	46%	.272
2019	HOU	MLB	35	8	1	0	10	10	62^2	58	6	1.3	7.5	52	52%	.289
2019	ARI	MLB	35	10	4	0	23	23	146	117	15	1.3	8.3	135	44%	.263
2020	HOU	MLB	36	14	6	0	29	29	175	158	27	1.9	8.6	166	46%	.277

Comparables: Javier Vazquez, Justin Verlander, Mike Mussina

Greinke is a work of art. He throws changeups faster than his fastball. He throws curveballs so slow he makes you believe you, too, could be in the big leagues. His grunts keep you on the edge of your seat. He's not going to strike out a ton of hitters, but he's going to throw all five of his pitches exactly where he wants to. He still plays Gold Glove defense, and it's an absolute shame he plays in the AL where we will be deprived of 36-year-old Greinke dingers. Houston could, and probably would, have been World Series favorites with or without Greinke, but that ring was too enticing not to go for it. When the Astros traded for him it signaled two things: Number 1, they were not content to simply be among the best teams in baseball this year, they wanted to be the clear-cut favorites. And the Number 2 should always be followed by washing your hands.

YEAR	TEAM	LVL	AGE	WHIP	ERA	DRA	WARP	MPH	FB%	WHF	CSP
2017	ARI	MLB	33	1.07	3.20	2.77	6.3	92.6	48.4	13.4	40.9
2018	ARI	MLB	34	1.08	3.21	3.09	5.3	91.8	48.7	11.7	45.1
2019	HOU	MLB	35	1.07	3.02	3.52	1.5	92.2	47.7	11.7	46.7
2019	ARI	MLB	35	0.95	2.90	3.06	4.3	91.9	47.7	11	47.5
2020	HOU	MLB	36	1.11	3.33	3.48	4.0	90.8	47.2	11.7	44

Zack Greinke, continued

Pitch Shape vs LHH

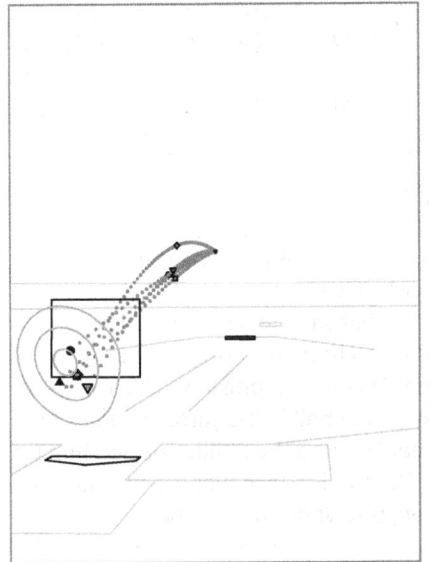

Pitch Shape vs RHH

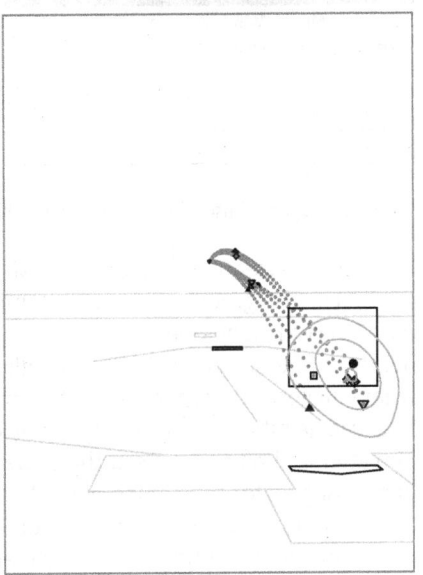

Type	Frequency	Velocity	H Movement	V Movement
● Fastball	41.1%	90.1 [93]	-1.4 [124]	-15.5 [101]
☐ Sinker	6.5%	90.1 [87]	-11.3 [109]	-20.8 [98]
+ Cutter				
▲ Changeup	20.8%	87.5 [108]	-10.5 [103]	-28.3 [97]
✕ Splitter				
▽ Slider	14.7%	83.7 [97]	6.6 [107]	-34.5 [96]
◇ Curveball	13.6%	70.7 [74]	11.3 [115]	-59.2 [75]
⊕ Slow Curveball				
✳ Knuckleball				
▼ Screwball				

Jared Hughes   RHP

Born: 07/04/85   Age: 34   Bats: R   Throws: R
Height: 6'7"   Weight: 240   Origin: Round 4, 2006 Draft (#110 overall)

YEAR	TEAM	LVL	AGE	W	L	SV	G	GS	IP	H	HR	BB/9	K/9	K	GB%	BABIP
2017	MIL	MLB	31	5	3	1	67	0	59^2	49	4	3.6	7.2	48	63%	.278
2018	CIN	MLB	32	4	3	7	72	0	78^2	57	4	2.6	6.8	59	66%	.252
2019	PHI	MLB	33	2	1	0	25	0	23	16	7	3.1	7.8	20	55%	.164
2019	CIN	MLB	33	3	4	1	47	0	48^1	41	6	3.5	6.3	34	63%	.254
2020	PHI	MLB	34	2	2	0	33	0	35	33	4	3.5	7.4	29	61%	.284

Comparables: Jim Johnson, Pedro Beato, Rob Scahill

It doesn't matter how "juiced" the ball is, you can't allow home runs if you keep the ball on the ground. This makes eminent sense in theory, but in practice didn't serve Hughes well last season, a year that saw the grizzled sinkerballer nearly double his previous career high of seven homers allowed. What you see is what you get with Hughes, a pitcher managers love despite low strikeout rates because he hits the zone and typically keeps the ball in the yard. The Reds cut him after finding no takers at the trade deadline and the Phillies picked him up in mid-August for their failed playoff run. Hughes is a face that blends into the crowd of the modern eight-pitcher bullpen, but whose durability and flexibility makes him an essential cog for any team.

YEAR	TEAM	LVL	AGE	WHIP	ERA	DRA	WARP	MPH	FB%	WHF	CSP
2017	MIL	MLB	31	1.22	3.02	5.86	-0.5	95.5	77.4	12.5	41.9
2018	CIN	MLB	32	1.02	1.94	4.59	0.3	94.0	86	12.8	42.2
2019	PHI	MLB	33	1.04	3.91	4.55	0.2	93.3	80	12.1	36.9
2019	CIN	MLB	33	1.24	4.10	4.64	0.4	93.2	81.1	10.1	37.8
2020	PHI	MLB	34	1.33	4.06	4.15	0.5	92.9	80.6	11.7	39.6

Jared Hughes, continued

Pitch Shape vs LHH

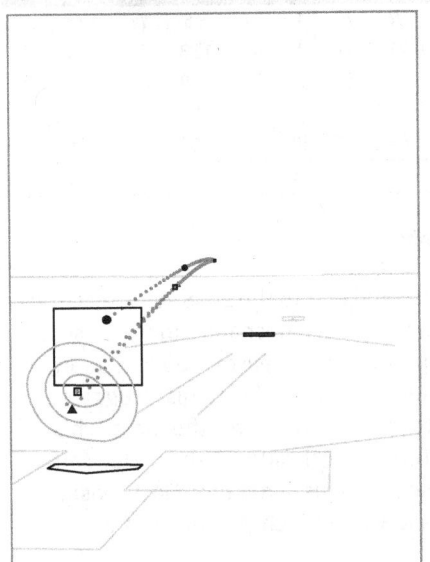

Pitch Shape vs RHH

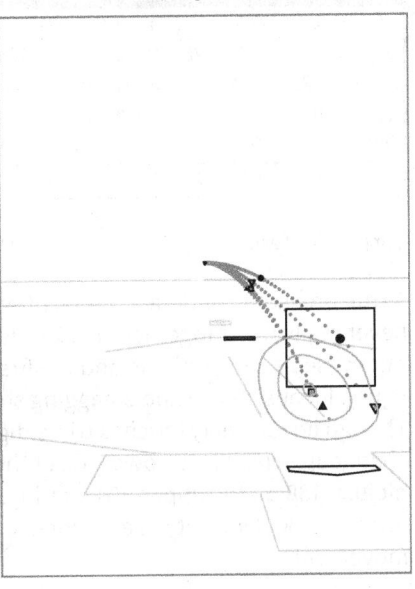

Type	Frequency	Velocity	H Movement	V Movement
● Fastball	5.9%	93.1 [102]	-10.6 [83]	-19.7 [90]
□ Sinker	74.8%	91.5 [94]	-13.8 [92]	-30.1 [66]
+ Cutter				
▲ Changeup	8.0%	84.8 [98]	-9 [110]	-31.6 [88]
✕ Splitter				
▽ Slider	11.3%	82.5 [92]	4.8 [99]	-36.5 [90]
◇ Curveball				
⊕ Slow Curveball				
✱ Knuckleball				
▼ Screwball				

Houston Astros 2020

Josh James RHP

Born: 03/08/93   Age: 27   Bats: R   Throws: R
Height: 6'3"   Weight: 206   Origin: Round 34, 2014 Draft (#1006 overall)

YEAR	TEAM	LVL	AGE	W	L	SV	G	GS	IP	H	HR	BB/9	K/9	K	GB%	BABIP
2017	CCH	AA	24	4	8	3	21	11	76	79	1	3.8	8.5	72	53%	.338
2018	CCH	AA	25	0	0	1	6	4	21^2	17	1	4.2	15.8	38	58%	.364
2018	FRE	AAA	25	6	4	0	17	17	92^2	62	8	3.8	12.9	133	41%	.278
2018	HOU	MLB	25	2	0	0	6	3	23	15	3	2.7	11.3	29	42%	.240
2019	HOU	MLB	26	5	1	1	49	1	61^1	46	10	5.1	14.7	100	35%	.308
2020	HOU	MLB	27	7	5	0	63	13	100	79	14	4.3	13.7	153	38%	.312

Comparables: Sean Poppen, Wander Suero, Brad Boxberger

A true breakout candidate after a phenomenal end to the 2018 season, James never really put it together in 2019. He tweaked his mechanics in the offseason but missed spring training and the first month of the season due to a quad injury. Inconsistency and a nagging shoulder injury added to his struggles. Though he routinely touches triple digits, the pitch he loves the most is his changeup, which he throws 20% of the time to both sides of the plate. Batters hit just .138 on the upper-80s offering. He threw his slider more last season, losing a tick of velocity in exchange for a few more inches of horizontal movement.

When he's on, that three-pitch mix is borderline unhittable. The problem is he hasn't shown the consistency needed to be a starter. He's got the raw stuff of a top of the rotation guy, but the command of a middle reliever. Whether that means he ends up as a back-of-the-rotation guy or a back-of-the-bullpen guy or something in between remains to be seen. There's a hole after the top three in the Astros rotation, so James will have his shot, but either way the Astros have a live arm they found in the 34th round.

YEAR	TEAM	LVL	AGE	WHIP	ERA	DRA	WARP	MPH	FB%	WHF	CSP
2017	CCH	AA	24	1.46	4.38	5.11	-0.1				
2018	CCH	AA	25	1.25	2.49	2.93	0.6				
2018	FRE	AAA	25	1.09	3.40	2.47	3.2				
2018	HOU	MLB	25	0.96	2.35	3.20	0.5	100.2	59.9	14.6	46.7
2019	HOU	MLB	26	1.32	4.70	3.36	1.3	99.3	63.3	16.6	46.4
2020	HOU	MLB	27	1.26	3.76	3.68	1.9	99.0	63.4	16.4	47.1

Josh James, continued

Pitch Shape vs LHH

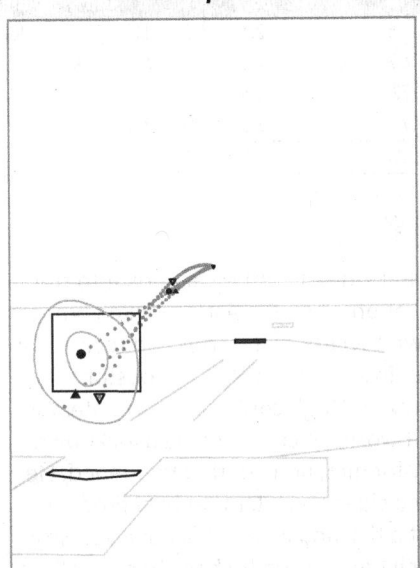

Pitch Shape vs RHH

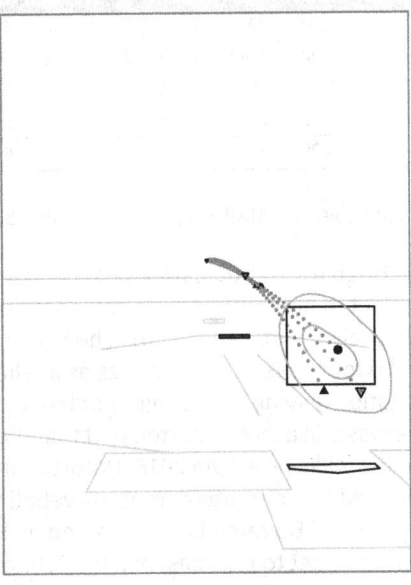

Type	Frequency	Velocity	H Movement	V Movement
● Fastball	63.3%	97.4 [114]	-7.2 [98]	-11.9 [110]
☐ Sinker				
+ Cutter				
▲ Changeup	14.6%	89.3 [115]	-14.3 [85]	-29.2 [95]
✕ Splitter				
▽ Slider	21.3%	84.6 [101]	11.3 [126]	-38 [86]
◇ Curveball				
⬥ Slow Curveball				
✳ Knuckleball				
▼ Screwball				

Collin McHugh RHP

Born: 06/19/87   Age: 33   Bats: R   Throws: R
Height: 6'2"   Weight: 190   Origin: Round 18, 2008 Draft (#554 overall)

YEAR	TEAM	LVL	AGE	W	L	SV	G	GS	IP	H	HR	BB/9	K/9	K	GB%	BABIP
2017	CCH	AA	30	0	0	0	4	4	15	18	1	2.4	6.6	11	57%	.340
2017	HOU	MLB	30	5	2	0	12	12	63^1	62	7	2.8	8.8	62	33%	.312
2018	HOU	MLB	31	6	2	0	58	0	72^1	45	6	2.6	11.7	94	35%	.248
2019	HOU	MLB	32	4	5	0	35	8	74^2	62	12	3.6	9.9	82	40%	.265
2020	*HOU*	*MLB*	*33*	*2*	*2*	*0*	*33*	*0*	*35*	*31*	*6*	*3.2*	*9.5*	*37*	*38%*	*.278*

Comparables: Kris Medlen, Carlos Carrasco, Mike Bolsinger

McHugh was set up perfectly to choose what kind of journey he took into the sunset of his career. After a career revitalization when the Astros picked him off the waiver wire heap in 2014, he had shown success as a starter and received a solid four days of All-Star buzz as a reliever in 2018. With 60% of Houston's rotation leaving due to injury or free agency, McHugh could show other teams he was still a viable starter, or if that didn't work, he could still be a lockdown reliever like he was in 2018. Unfortunately for him, none of that happened. He ditched his spin-rate-darling curveball for a sidearm slider that backfired all year. His K:BB rate plummeted and he lost a tick and a half of fastball velocity. He'll still get to play baseball in 2020, which I'm sure would have been thrilling to know back in 2013 with a double-digit ERA, but it seems he hit free agency one year too late.

YEAR	TEAM	LVL	AGE	WHIP	ERA	DRA	WARP	MPH	FB%	WHF	CSP
2017	CCH	AA	30	1.47	3.60	5.78	-0.1				
2017	HOU	MLB	30	1.29	3.55	4.58	0.7	92.1	50.6	13.2	48.4
2018	HOU	MLB	31	0.91	1.99	2.70	1.9	93.8	49.6	14.1	47.1
2019	HOU	MLB	32	1.23	4.70	4.94	0.5	92.7	33.4	12.2	46.8
2020	*HOU*	*MLB*	*33*	*1.23*	*4.00*	*4.09*	*0.4*	*91.9*	*42.1*	*12.9*	*46.7*

Collin McHugh, continued

Pitch Shape vs LHH

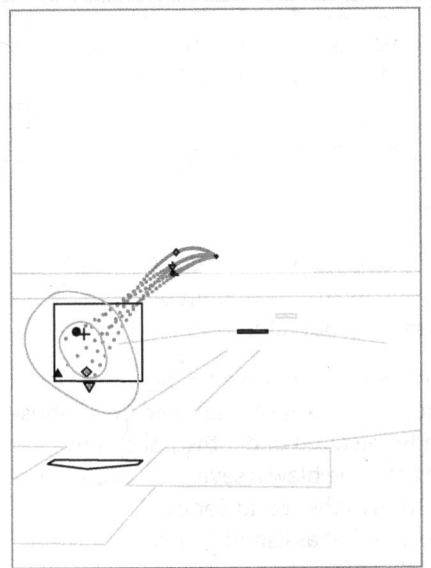

Pitch Shape vs RHH

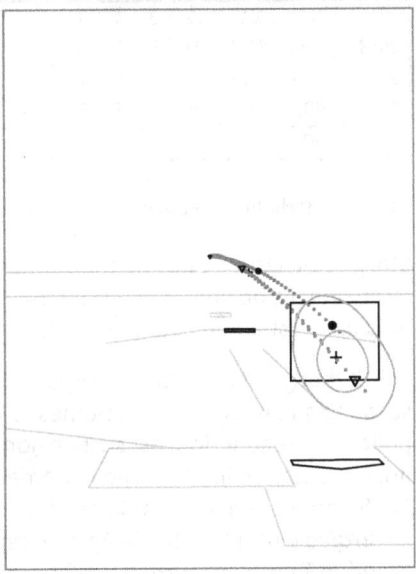

Type	Frequency	Velocity	H Movement	V Movement
● Fastball	32.6%	91.1 [96]	-8.7 [92]	-15.5 [101]
☐ Sinker				
+ Cutter	12.1%	87.3 [91]	2.3 [103]	-25.5 [95]
▲ Changeup	3.1%	84.3 [96]	-12.5 [94]	-28.1 [98]
✕ Splitter				
▽ Slider	43.3%	79.8 [81]	15.2 [143]	-38.7 [84]
◇ Curveball	8.1%	74.8 [88]	12.5 [121]	-55.1 [84]
✥ Slow Curveball				
✳ Knuckleball				
▼ Screwball				

Houston Astros 2020

Roberto Osuna   RHP

Born: 02/07/95   Age: 25   Bats: R   Throws: R
Height: 6'2"   Weight: 215   Origin: International Free Agent, 2011

YEAR	TEAM	LVL	AGE	W	L	SV	G	GS	IP	H	HR	BB/9	K/9	K	GB%	BABIP
2017	TOR	MLB	22	3	4	39	66	0	64	46	3	1.3	11.7	83	47%	.285
2018	TOR	MLB	23	0	0	9	15	0	15^1	16	0	0.6	7.6	13	40%	.340
2018	HOU	MLB	23	2	2	12	23	0	22^2	17	1	1.2	7.5	19	44%	.258
2019	HOU	MLB	24	4	3	38	66	0	65	45	8	1.7	10.1	73	40%	.234
2020	HOU	MLB	25	3	3	44	61	0	64	50	8	2.4	10.7	76	40%	.275

Comparables: Huston Street, Kelvin Herrera, Neftalí Feliz

Still just 24, Osuna became the youngest player ever to record 150 saves. Interestingly, he does it without striking out an absurd amount of hitters, finishing 61st among qualified relievers in strikeout rate.

But that's not really the story, is it? Last season, he served a 75-game suspension under the Joint Domestic Violence, Sexual Assault and Child Abuse policy, the second-longest suspension administered under the policy since its implementation in 2015. Then, moments after he blew a save in an eventual ALCS Game 6 win that would send the Astros to the World Series, *Sports Illustrated* writer Stephanie Apstein reported that assistant general manager Brandon Taubman "turned to a group of three female reporters, including one wearing a purple domestic-violence awareness bracelet, and yelled, half a dozen times, "Thank God we got Osuna! I'm so f- - - glad we got Osuna!" After increasingly pathetic attempts to deny or downplay the events, the Astros eventually fired Taubman.

www.hawc.org/donate

YEAR	TEAM	LVL	AGE	WHIP	ERA	DRA	WARP	MPH	FB%	WHF	CSP
2017	TOR	MLB	22	0.86	3.38	2.41	2.0	96.4	48	17.6	41.9
2018	TOR	MLB	23	1.11	2.93	3.97	0.2	97.5	67.7	13.4	50.5
2018	HOU	MLB	23	0.88	1.99	3.54	0.4	96.9	67.7	16.9	48.3
2019	HOU	MLB	24	0.88	2.63	3.53	1.3	98.6	49.3	18.4	46.6
2020	HOU	MLB	25	1.05	2.78	2.96	1.6	97.3	54.2	17.9	47.4

Roberto Osuna, continued

Pitch Shape vs LHH

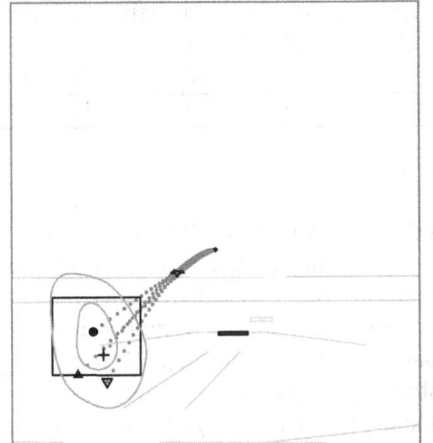

Pitch Shape vs RHH

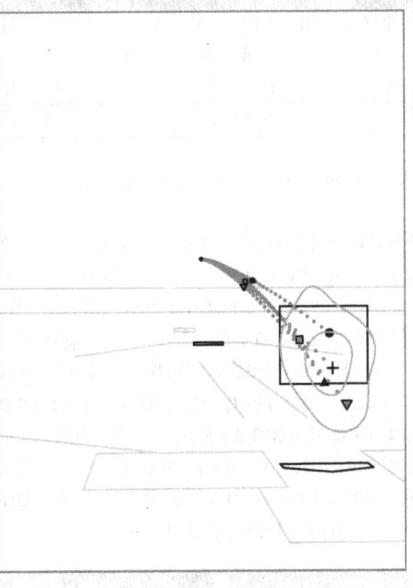

Type	Frequency	Velocity	H Movement	V Movement
● Fastball	44.8%	96.9 [113]	-4.9 [109]	-10 [116]
□ Sinker	4.5%	96.1 [118]	-10.3 [115]	-12.4 [128]
+ Cutter	15.2%	91.5 [118]	5 [119]	-20.3 [114]
▲ Changeup	18.6%	84.6 [98]	-11.7 [98]	-23.7 [111]
✕ Splitter				
▽ Slider	17.0%	88.1 [116]	6.4 [106]	-28.7 [113]
◇ Curveball				
✦ Slow Curveball				
✳ Knuckleball				
▼ Screwball				

Brad Peacock RHP

Born: 02/02/88 Age: 32 Bats: R Throws: R
Height: 6'1" Weight: 210 Origin: Round 41, 2006 Draft (#1231 overall)

YEAR	TEAM	LVL	AGE	W	L	SV	G	GS	IP	H	HR	BB/9	K/9	K	GB%	BABIP
2017	HOU	MLB	29	13	2	0	34	21	132	100	10	3.9	11.0	161	44%	.286
2018	HOU	MLB	30	3	5	3	61	1	65	56	11	2.8	13.3	96	37%	.317
2019	HOU	MLB	31	7	6	0	23	15	91²	78	15	3.0	9.4	96	38%	.267
2020	HOU	MLB	32	8	6	0	55	16	123	117	22	3.8	10.1	138	39%	.300

Comparables: P.J. Walters, Fernando Nieve, Cody Martin

Peacock's past few seasons have mirrored his two-seam and slider pitch mix, yo-yoing back and forth from the rotation to the bullpen. It's too bad Jake Mintz of the Céspedes Family BBQ already has dibs on "America's ROOGY" because Peacock would be in the running with his utter dominance of same-handed foes—he finished with the second-best batting average allowed (.179) to righties in 2019. Last year, we said his days as a starting pitcher are over; then he went out and started 15 games so what do we know? He'll probably [side eyes the 2019 Annual] never replicate his 2017 season when he became the de facto Staff Ace for a good chunk of the season, but there's still value in his arm, no matter what inning he's pitching in.

YEAR	TEAM	LVL	AGE	WHIP	ERA	DRA	WARP	MPH	FB%	WHF	CSP
2017	HOU	MLB	29	1.19	3.00	2.91	3.8	94.3	51.3	12.9	47.8
2018	HOU	MLB	30	1.17	3.46	2.54	1.8	94.9	54.6	13.9	45.4
2019	HOU	MLB	31	1.19	4.12	5.11	0.6	94.1	58.5	9.4	47.7
2020	HOU	MLB	32	1.37	4.81	4.70	1.0	93.4	54.5	11.6	46.5

Brad Peacock, continued

Pitch Shape vs LHH	Pitch Shape vs RHH
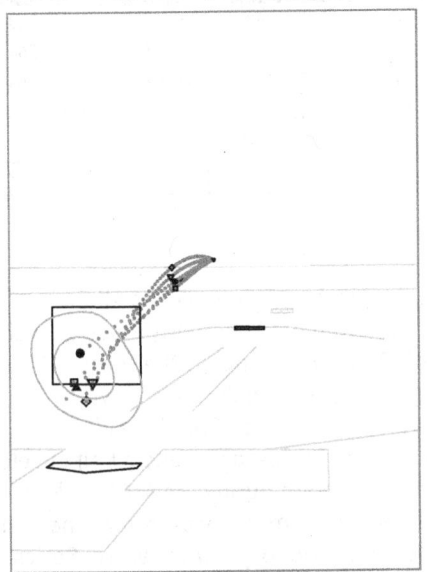	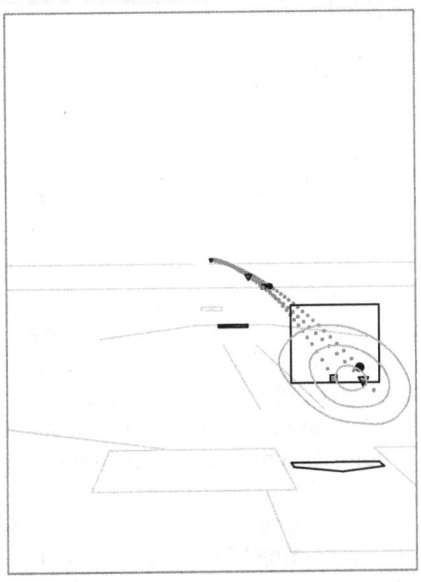

Type	Frequency	Velocity	H Movement	V Movement
● Fastball	27.8%	92.8 [101]	-11.4 [80]	-15.6 [101]
☐ Sinker	30.7%	92 [97]	-16.2 [77]	-21.9 [95]
+ Cutter				
▲ Changeup	5.9%	83.6 [94]	-15.8 [78]	-30.6 [91]
✕ Splitter				
▽ Slider	28.6%	81.5 [88]	12.3 [130]	-30.8 [107]
◇ Curveball	7.0%	78.8 [101]	10.9 [114]	-50.3 [94]
⊕ Slow Curveball				
✳ Knuckleball				
▼ Screwball				

Houston Astros 2020

Ryan Pressly   RHP
Born: 12/15/88   Age: 31   Bats: R   Throws: R
Height: 6'3"   Weight: 210   Origin: Round 11, 2007 Draft (#354 overall)

YEAR	TEAM	LVL	AGE	W	L	SV	G	GS	IP	H	HR	BB/9	K/9	K	GB%	BABIP
2017	ROC	AAA	28	2	0	4	7	0	10	5	0	4.5	13.5	15	55%	.250
2017	MIN	MLB	28	2	3	0	57	0	61^1	52	10	2.8	9.0	61	52%	.264
2018	MIN	MLB	29	1	1	0	51	0	47^2	46	5	3.6	13.0	69	50%	.363
2018	HOU	MLB	29	1	0	2	26	0	23^1	11	1	1.2	12.3	32	62%	.213
2019	HOU	MLB	30	2	3	3	55	0	54^1	37	6	2.0	11.9	72	52%	.258
2020	HOU	MLB	31	3	3	8	61	0	64	55	8	3.0	11.9	85	50%	.312

Comparables: Kevin Jepsen, Mel Rojas, Mike Adams

How good does one have to be that a season in which they make an All-Star team and have a 2.32 ERA feels like a disappointment? Apparently Pressly-level good. He didn't even give up a run until his 20th appearance of the season. A freak knee injury limited him to just 10 appearances after July and he was clearly a shell of himself in the postseason, but even "bad" Pressly held opponents scoreless in nine of those ten outings. He lost a tick and a half of velo on all of his pitches down the stretch and at one point during the ALCS looked like his knee came unglued from his thigh, only for him to say post-game he had been expecting that for weeks and he would be good to go for the World Series. Professional athletes are crazy. Assuming he's healthy in 2020, look for him to spin hitters dizzy with his hammer curve and power slider. He has quickly blossomed into one of the game's upper-echelon relievers.

YEAR	TEAM	LVL	AGE	WHIP	ERA	DRA	WARP	MPH	FB%	WHF	CSP
2017	ROC	AAA	28	1.00	0.90	2.81	0.3				
2017	MIN	MLB	28	1.16	4.70	3.48	1.2	97.8	55	13.4	49.4
2018	MIN	MLB	29	1.36	3.40	1.97	1.6	98.1	48.6	19.4	47.2
2018	HOU	MLB	29	0.60	0.77	1.73	0.9	97.6	34.7	17.7	47.6
2019	HOU	MLB	30	0.90	2.32	2.60	1.6	97.3	35.7	18.3	46.7
2020	HOU	MLB	31	1.19	3.30	3.33	1.3	96.8	43.6	17.2	47.3

Ryan Pressly, continued

Pitch Shape vs LHH	Pitch Shape vs RHH
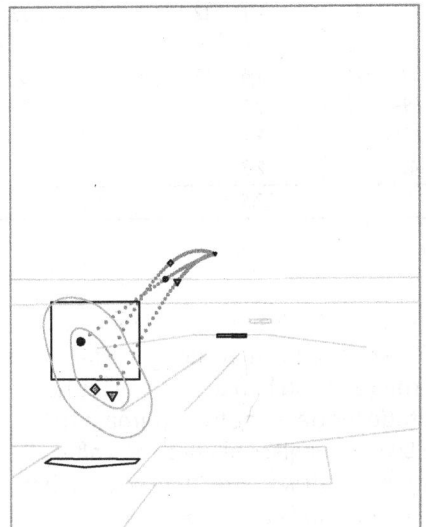	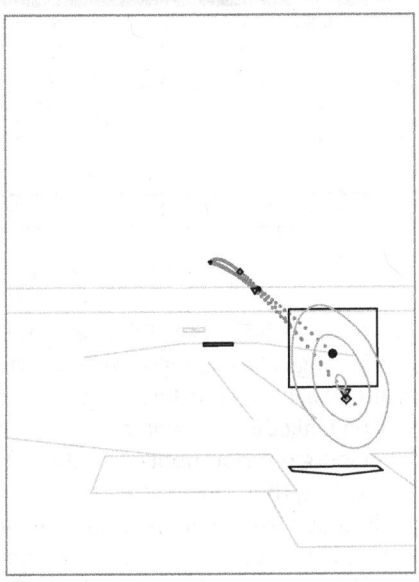

Type	Frequency	Velocity	H Movement	V Movement
● Fastball	35.7%	95.8 [110]	-2.2 [121]	-11.8 [111]
☐ Sinker				
+ Cutter				
▲ Changeup				
✕ Splitter				
▽ Slider	29.2%	90.3 [125]	4.9 [99]	-27.9 [115]
◇ Curveball	35.2%	83.1 [115]	15 [131]	-46.9 [102]
✦ Slow Curveball				
✱ Knuckleball				
▼ Screwball				

Austin Pruitt RHP

Born: 08/31/89 Age: 30 Bats: R Throws: R
Height: 5'10" Weight: 185 Origin: Round 9, 2013 Draft (#278 overall)

YEAR	TEAM	LVL	AGE	W	L	SV	G	GS	IP	H	HR	BB/9	K/9	K	GB%	BABIP
2017	DUR	AAA	27	0	1	1	9	4	24^2	17	2	0.7	12.0	33	58%	.273
2017	TBA	MLB	27	7	5	1	30	8	83	103	11	2.4	7.2	66	46%	.345
2018	DUR	AAA	28	3	0	1	14	4	39^2	26	2	1.6	11.1	49	49%	.261
2018	TBA	MLB	28	2	3	4	23	0	69^2	72	7	2.1	5.4	42	50%	.289
2019	DUR	AAA	29	3	3	0	18	6	48^1	61	9	2.2	9.5	51	49%	.364
2019	TBA	MLB	29	3	0	0	14	2	47	47	7	2.3	7.5	39	55%	.296
2020	TBA	MLB	30	1	1	0	24	0	26	26	4	2.5	7.5	21	49%	.295

Comparables: Seth Lugo, Brent Suter, Josh Lueke

Do you know how some things are still around in 2020 and you do not know why? Things like wiping ourselves with paper, sending information via fax or Pruitt on a 40-man roster? Those type of things. If you had to endorse his best skill on LinkedIn, you would note his aptitude for traveling from Durham to St. Petersburg on short notice and throwing 50 meaningless pitches soon after. Meanwhile, there was a stretch when the Rays' staff was stretched so thin that Pruitt made two meaningful starts in late August and early September. He allowed just two runs across them combined, but then was used just twice the rest of the season when more dynamic arms were available. It has been a mystifying, magical ride thus far, but with 40-man roster spots becoming scarce this may be the last stop on the Pruitt Express.

YEAR	TEAM	LVL	AGE	WHIP	ERA	DRA	WARP	MPH	FB%	WHF	CSP
2017	DUR	AAA	27	0.77	2.55	2.06	0.9				
2017	TBA	MLB	27	1.51	5.31	4.81	0.5	93.2	43.3	10.4	47.1
2018	DUR	AAA	28	0.83	2.95	2.35	1.3				
2018	TBA	MLB	28	1.26	4.65	3.66	1.0	93.8	44	10.3	50.6
2019	DUR	AAA	29	1.51	5.40	5.09	0.6				
2019	TBA	MLB	29	1.26	4.40	4.76	0.3	93.5	44	11.9	46.9
2020	TBA	MLB	30	1.28	4.02	4.31	0.2	92.8	43.6	10.8	48

Austin Pruitt, continued

Pitch Shape vs LHH

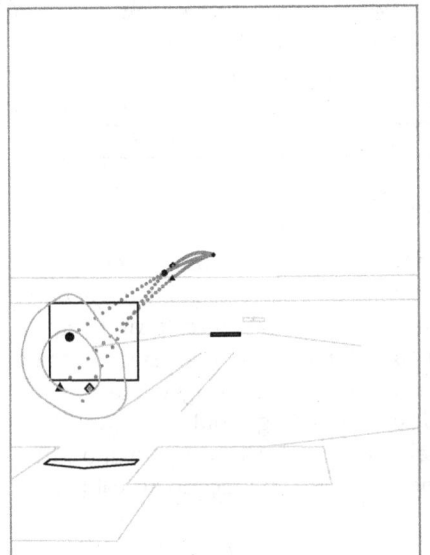

Pitch Shape vs RHH

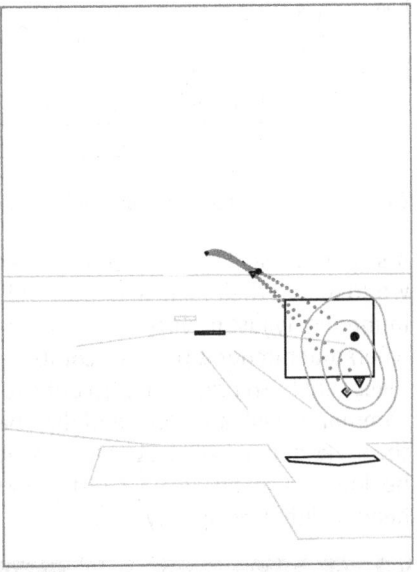

Type	Frequency	Velocity	H Movement	V Movement
● Fastball	43.1%	92.2 [99]	-1.1 [125]	-15.2 [102]
☐ Sinker				
+ Cutter				
▲ Changeup	19.2%	86.4 [104]	-9.7 [107]	-26 [104]
✕ Splitter				
▽ Slider	23.5%	87.6 [114]	4.6 [99]	-31.1 [106]
◇ Curveball	13.3%	81.8 [111]	6.5 [96]	-45 [105]
✤ Slow Curveball				
✳ Knuckleball				
▼ Screwball				

Astros Player Analysis - 73

Aaron Sanchez RHP

Born: 07/01/92 Age: 27 Bats: R Throws: R
Height: 6'4" Weight: 210 Origin: Round 1, 2010 Draft (#34 overall)

YEAR	TEAM	LVL	AGE	W	L	SV	G	GS	IP	H	HR	BB/9	K/9	K	GB%	BABIP
2017	TOR	MLB	24	1	3	0	8	8	36	42	6	5.0	6.0	24	48%	.310
2018	TOR	MLB	25	4	6	0	20	20	105	106	11	5.0	7.4	86	50%	.304
2019	HOU	MLB	26	2	0	0	4	4	18^2	14	5	4.3	7.7	16	47%	.180
2019	TOR	MLB	26	3	14	0	23	23	112^2	131	15	4.7	7.9	99	48%	.341
2020	HOU	MLB	27	2	2	0	33	0	35	37	5	4.6	7.9	31	49%	.311

Comparables: Randall Delgado, Eduardo Rodriguez, Archie Bradley

It's got to be jarring for a team to make a trade with the Astros and the entire world to nod their head in unison while saying that player is going to get better immediately just by virtue of not being on your team anymore. It can't help when that pitcher is part of a combined no-hitter in his very first start. But hot takes that burn brightest burn out the fastest as Sanchez struggled to command, well, anything, and then had season-ending shoulder surgery. From the looks of it, he will be out for a good chunk of next season, too. If and when he does return, he will have just a few months to try and recoup his value before heading into free agency.

YEAR	TEAM	LVL	AGE	WHIP	ERA	DRA	WARP	MPH	FB%	WHF	CSP
2017	TOR	MLB	24	1.72	4.25	7.30	-0.7	97.3	76.9	6.5	44.7
2018	TOR	MLB	25	1.56	4.89	5.97	-0.8	96.4	64.5	10.5	44.9
2019	HOU	MLB	26	1.23	4.82	2.89	0.6	94.1	53.8	10.8	46.1
2019	TOR	MLB	26	1.69	6.07	7.40	-2.0	96.2	58.3	9.6	46.9
2020	HOU	MLB	27	1.58	5.56	5.17	0.0	95.7	62.5	9.9	46.2

Aaron Sanchez, continued

Pitch Shape vs LHH	Pitch Shape vs RHH
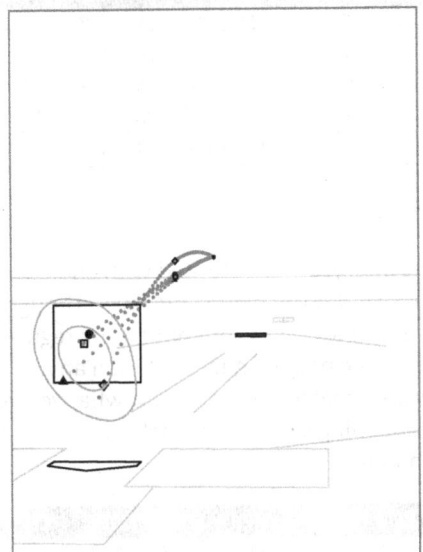	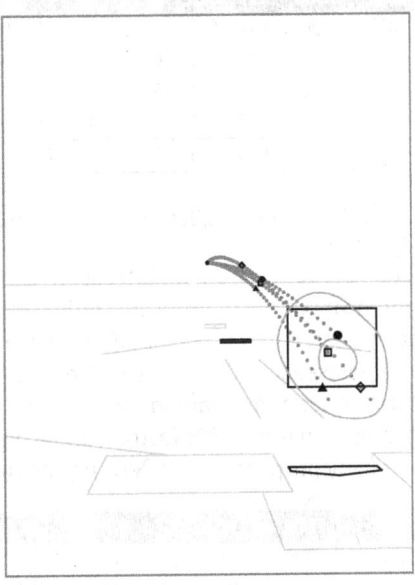

Type	Frequency	Velocity	H Movement	V Movement
● Fastball	24.3%	93.7 [104]	-11.6 [79]	-15.2 [102]
☐ Sinker	33.4%	94.2 [108]	-14.3 [89]	-17.5 [110]
+ Cutter				
▲ Changeup	19.4%	88.4 [111]	-15 [82]	-25.9 [104]
✕ Splitter				
▽ Slider				
◇ Curveball	23.0%	78.7 [100]	13.3 [123]	-51.9 [91]
⊕ Slow Curveball				
✳ Knuckleball				
▼ Screwball				

Astros Player Analysis - 75

Houston Astros 2020

Joe Smith   RHP

Born: 03/22/84   Age: 36   Bats: R   Throws: R
Height: 6'2"   Weight: 205   Origin: Round 3, 2006 Draft (#94 overall)

YEAR	TEAM	LVL	AGE	W	L	SV	G	GS	IP	H	HR	BB/9	K/9	K	GB%	BABIP
2017	TOR	MLB	33	3	0	0	38	0	35^2	30	3	2.5	12.9	51	44%	.342
2017	CLE	MLB	33	0	0	1	21	0	18^1	16	1	0.0	9.8	20	60%	.306
2018	HOU	MLB	34	5	1	0	56	0	45^2	34	7	2.4	9.1	46	45%	.239
2019	HOU	MLB	35	1	0	0	28	0	25	19	2	1.8	7.9	22	49%	.254
2020	HOU	MLB	36	2	2	0	44	0	47	49	8	2.1	8.5	44	48%	.307

Comparables: Javy Guerra, Jeremy Jeffress, Hector Carrasco

After recovering from an offseason Achilles injury, Smith returned with enough side-arm arrows to prove he could still miss Styx at the big-league level. Though he appeared in less than half the season, Smith was lights out during the regular and postseason, especially in the ALCS where he had a higher WPA than any Astros pitcher not named Gerrit Cole. Thirteen seasons in, you know what you're getting—an upper-80s fastball and a big, sweeping slider with a delivery inversely proportional to how boring his name is.

YEAR	TEAM	LVL	AGE	WHIP	ERA	DRA	WARP	MPH	FB%	WHF	CSP
2017	TOR	MLB	33	1.12	3.28	3.28	0.8	91.0	67.7	13.4	52.8
2017	CLE	MLB	33	0.87	3.44	3.54	0.3	90.4	64.2	10.6	53.2
2018	HOU	MLB	34	1.01	3.74	4.49	0.2	89.9	65.1	11.2	50.5
2019	HOU	MLB	35	0.96	1.80	4.25	0.3	90.1	57.6	9.9	56.4
2020	HOU	MLB	36	1.29	4.70	4.69	0.3	89.0	62.4	11.1	52.4

Joe Smith, continued

Pitch Shape vs LHH

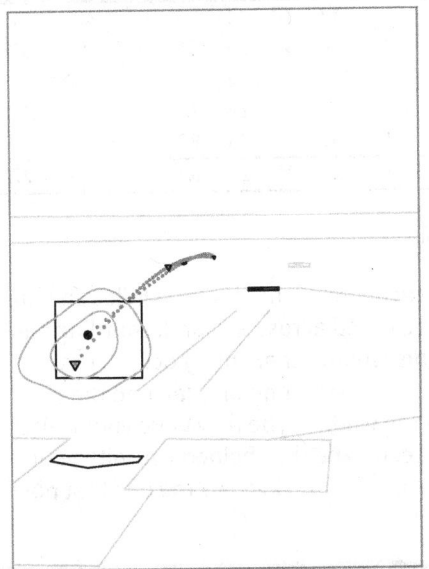

Pitch Shape vs RHH

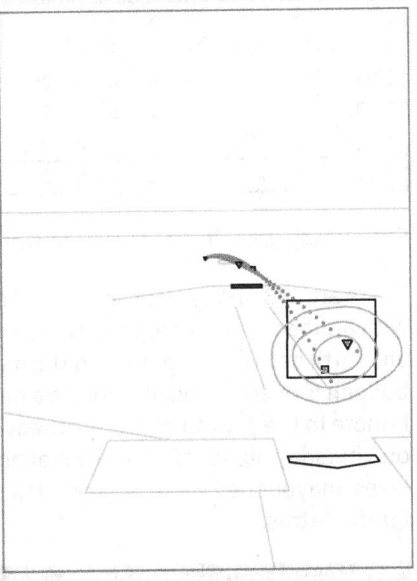

Type	Frequency	Velocity	H Movement	V Movement
● Fastball	25.3%	89.2 [91]	-16.4 [58]	-29.4 [65]
☐ Sinker	32.3%	87.4 [73]	-13.7 [93]	-39.9 [31]
+ Cutter				
▲ Changeup				
✕ Splitter				
▽ Slider	41.0%	79.6 [80]	11.5 [127]	-30.4 [108]
◇ Curveball				
✦ Slow Curveball				
✹ Knuckleball				
▼ Screwball				

Cy Sneed   RHP

Born: 10/01/92   Age: 27   Bats: R   Throws: R
Height: 6'4"   Weight: 215   Origin: Round 3, 2014 Draft (#85 overall)

YEAR	TEAM	LVL	AGE	W	L	SV	G	GS	IP	H	HR	BB/9	K/9	K	GB%	BABIP
2017	CCH	AA	24	9	5	1	22	14	97	117	12	3.1	7.5	81	47%	.345
2017	FRE	AAA	24	1	1	0	4	4	17^2	25	4	3.6	7.1	14	40%	.362
2018	FRE	AAA	25	10	6	0	26	20	127	120	6	3.8	8.1	114	46%	.315
2019	ROU	AAA	26	7	6	1	19	9	81^2	71	13	2.6	7.8	71	41%	.261
2019	HOU	MLB	26	0	1	0	8	0	21^1	26	5	2.1	9.7	23	48%	.350
2020	HOU	MLB	27	3	3	0	32	5	50	52	10	2.9	8.1	45	42%	.297

Comparables: Charles Brewer, Logan Verrett, Tyler Wilson

There are 143 anonymous, bearded American men who throw 94 miles an hour with a slider and a changeup. They can be found across the land, shuttling back and forth between Triple-A and the majors whenever an injury occurs, or the bullpen is overworked, or there is a doubleheader, or no one can find the remote to the TV. You might see them in the wild. Maybe they were your waiter on Thursday night at Outback Steakhouse, maybe they helped you with your taxes, maybe they are making the league minimum. Sneed is the one that plays for the Astros.

YEAR	TEAM	LVL	AGE	WHIP	ERA	DRA	WARP	MPH	FB%	WHF	CSP
2017	CCH	AA	24	1.55	5.01	5.76	-0.8				
2017	FRE	AAA	24	1.81	11.21	6.00	-0.1				
2018	FRE	AAA	25	1.36	3.83	4.13	2.0				
2019	ROU	AAA	26	1.16	4.19	2.89	2.9				
2019	HOU	MLB	26	1.45	5.48	5.23	0.0	94.8	69.8	11.6	50.7
2020	HOU	MLB	27	1.37	4.93	4.82	0.3	94.3	70.6	11.8	51.3

Cy Sneed, continued

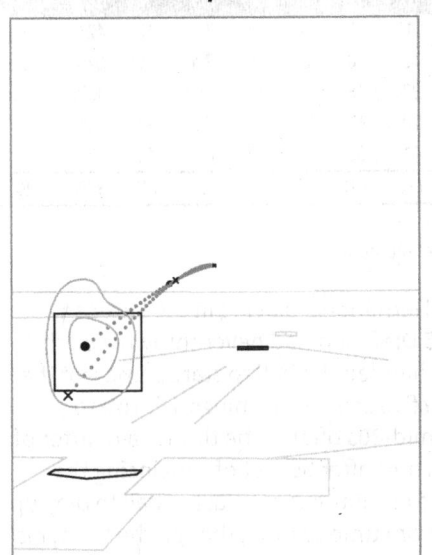

Pitch Shape vs LHH

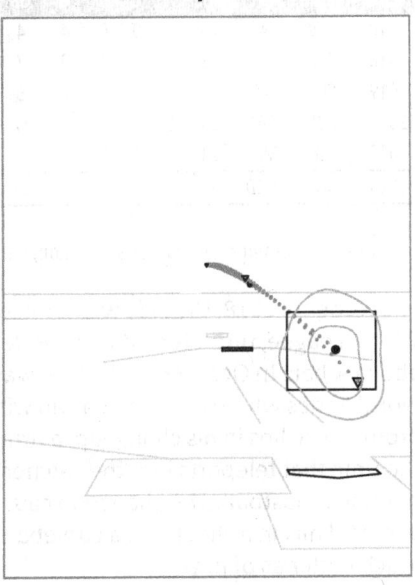

Pitch Shape vs RHH

Type	Frequency	Velocity	H Movement	V Movement
● Fastball	69.8%	92.5 [100]	1.3 [136]	-14.4 [104]
☐ Sinker				
+ Cutter				
▲ Changeup				
✕ Splitter	11.3%	79.6 [76]	-1.1 [125]	-31.3 [93]
▽ Slider	11.9%	82.4 [91]	8.2 [113]	-32.1 [103]
◇ Curveball	7.0%	79.4 [102]	7.7 [101]	-49.5 [96]
⊕ Slow Curveball				
✳ Knuckleball				
▼ Screwball				

Jose Urquidy RHP

Born: 05/01/95 Age: 25 Bats: R Throws: R
Height: 6'0" Weight: 180 Origin: International Free Agent, 2015

YEAR	TEAM	LVL	AGE	W	L	SV	G	GS	IP	H	HR	BB/9	K/9	K	GB%	BABIP
2018	TCV	A-	23	0	0	0	4	4	11¹	15	0	1.6	7.9	10	42%	.395
2018	BCA	A+	23	2	2	0	9	7	46	40	2	1.6	7.4	38	52%	.281
2019	CCH	AA	24	2	2	0	7	6	33	28	2	1.4	10.9	40	43%	.302
2019	ROU	AAA	24	5	3	0	13	12	70	67	15	2.1	12.1	94	34%	.311
2019	HOU	MLB	24	2	1	0	9	7	41	38	6	1.5	8.8	40	38%	.281
2020	HOU	MLB	25	9	5	0	21	21	112	101	17	2.6	9.0	112	37%	.282

Comparables: Domingo Germán, Jharel Cotton, Rafael Montero

In October of 2018, Urquidy was named Hernández, playing in the Mexican Winter League, unprotected in the Rule 5 Draft and had never thrown a pitch above A-ball. In October of 2019, he was handed the ball to start Game 4 of the World Series where he earned a win with five scoreless innings. His rise to prominence lies in his changeup, a firm mid-80s offering he throws a quarter of the time that teleports into the catcher's mitt after 55 feet of convincing the hitter it's a fastball. The changeup causes his nothing-special fastball to play up and he'll mix in a slider and a curveball from time to time, though the former is much better as of now.

YEAR	TEAM	LVL	AGE	WHIP	ERA	DRA	WARP	MPH	FB%	WHF	CSP
2018	TCV	A-	23	1.50	2.38	5.83	-0.1				
2018	BCA	A+	23	1.04	2.35	3.26	1.1				
2019	CCH	AA	24	1.00	4.09	3.07	0.7				
2019	ROU	AAA	24	1.19	4.63	2.87	2.6				
2019	HOU	MLB	24	1.10	3.95	4.33	0.6	95.4	47.3	13	49.8
2020	HOU	MLB	25	1.20	3.73	3.81	2.2	95.1	48.5	13.3	51

Jose Urquidy, continued

Pitch Shape vs LHH

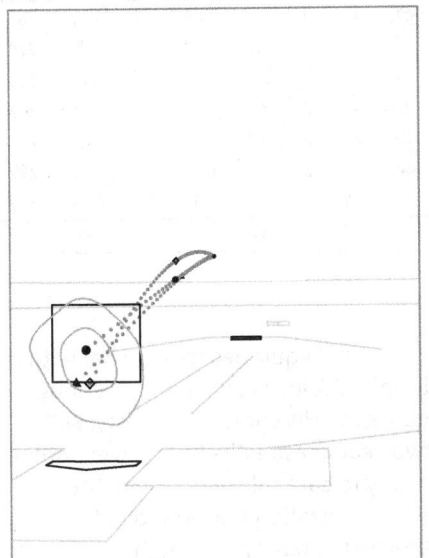

Pitch Shape vs RHH

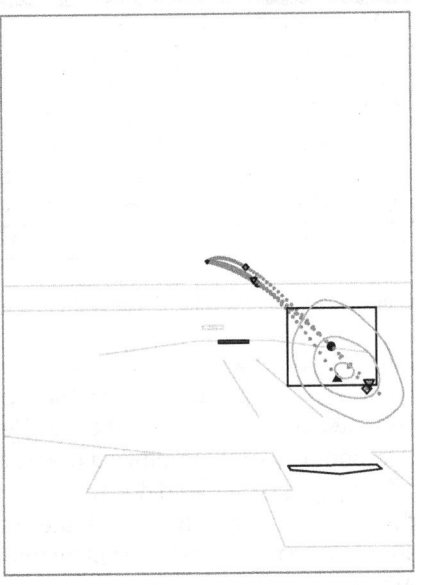

Type	Frequency	Velocity	H Movement	V Movement
● Fastball	47.3%	93.3 [103]	-8.1 [94]	-12.7 [109]
☐ Sinker				
+ Cutter				
▲ Changeup	25.4%	84.4 [97]	-14.2 [86]	-26.7 [102]
✕ Splitter				
▽ Slider	15.3%	83.3 [95]	4.3 [97]	-29.6 [110]
◇ Curveball	12.0%	79.1 [102]	7.4 [100]	-47.4 [100]
✥ Slow Curveball				
✱ Knuckleball				
▼ Screwball				

Houston Astros 2020

Framber Valdez   LHP
Born: 11/19/93   Age: 26   Bats: L   Throws: L
Height: 5'11"   Weight: 170   Origin: International Free Agent, 2015

YEAR	TEAM	LVL	AGE	W	L	SV	G	GS	IP	H	HR	BB/9	K/9	K	GB%	BABIP
2017	BCA	A+	23	2	3	1	13	9	61^1	41	3	4.3	10.7	73	57%	.257
2017	CCH	AA	23	5	5	0	12	9	49	60	4	4.2	9.7	53	60%	.394
2018	CCH	AA	24	4	5	1	20	13	94^1	92	7	2.8	11.4	120	58%	.363
2018	FRE	AAA	24	2	0	0	2	1	8^2	8	0	3.1	9.3	9	48%	.348
2018	HOU	MLB	24	4	1	0	8	5	37	22	3	5.8	8.3	34	71%	.213
2019	ROU	AAA	25	5	2	1	10	7	44^1	29	3	3.5	14.0	69	76%	.299
2019	HOU	MLB	25	4	7	0	26	8	70^2	74	9	5.6	8.7	68	62%	.319
2020	HOU	MLB	26	6	5	0	44	11	86	87	11	4.8	8.7	83	63%	.314

Comparables: Thomas Pannone, Matt Hall, Erick Fedde

What do you do with a command pitcher's arsenal equipped to a pitcher with no command? A big lefty with a bowling ball sinker, Valdez could not find enough consistency to be effective at the big league level. His curveball is nasty, with .186 and .188 xwOBAs allowed the past two years, respectively, but every other offering gets hammered due to his propensity to carefully place them directly down the middle of the plate. If there's any organization that would tell someone to throw their best pitch until they're beaten by it, though, it's the Astros.

YEAR	TEAM	LVL	AGE	WHIP	ERA	DRA	WARP	MPH	FB%	WHF	CSP
2017	BCA	A+	23	1.14	2.79	3.23	1.4				
2017	CCH	AA	23	1.69	5.88	6.60	-0.9				
2018	CCH	AA	24	1.28	4.10	4.04	1.3				
2018	FRE	AAA	24	1.27	4.15	4.03	0.1				
2018	HOU	MLB	24	1.24	2.19	6.12	-0.4	94.8	69	8.9	43.9
2019	ROU	AAA	25	1.04	3.25	1.35	2.3				
2019	HOU	MLB	25	1.67	5.86	5.70	-0.1	95.6	61.5	11.2	48.4
2020	HOU	MLB	26	1.55	5.13	4.83	0.6	95.0	64.9	10.6	47.2

Framber Valdez, continued

Pitch Shape vs LHH

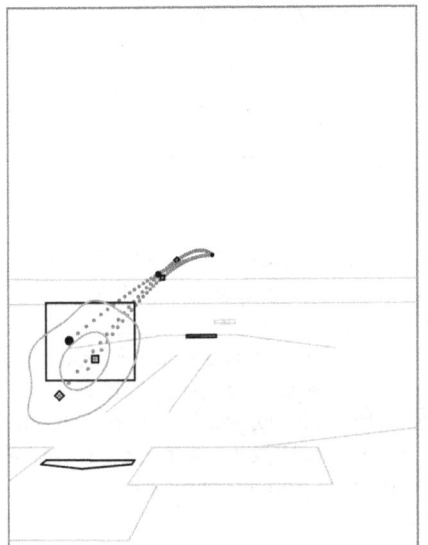

Pitch Shape vs RHH

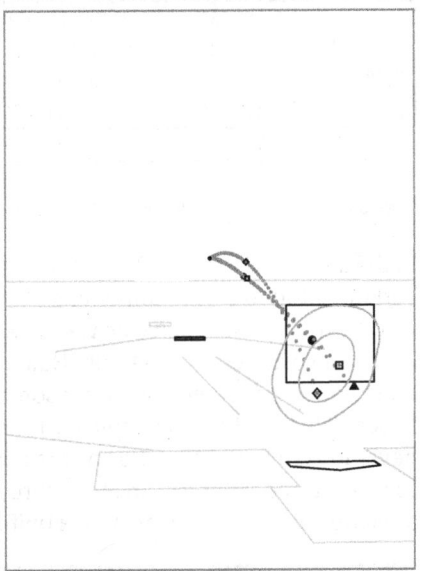

Type	Frequency	Velocity	H Movement	V Movement
● Fastball	18.2%	94.3 [106]	3.9 [113]	-17 [97]
□ Sinker	43.2%	92.6 [100]	11.2 [109]	-24.5 [86]
+ Cutter				
▲ Changeup	4.3%	88.4 [111]	11.8 [97]	-30.2 [92]
✕ Splitter				
▽ Slider				
◇ Curveball	34.2%	79.5 [103]	-11.6 [117]	-52.6 [89]
⊕ Slow Curveball				
✳ Knuckleball				
▼ Screwball				

Houston Astros 2020

Justin Verlander RHP

Born: 02/20/83   Age: 37   Bats: R   Throws: R
Height: 6'5"   Weight: 225   Origin: Round 1, 2004 Draft (#2 overall)

YEAR	TEAM	LVL	AGE	W	L	SV	G	GS	IP	H	HR	BB/9	K/9	K	GB%	BABIP
2017	DET	MLB	34	10	8	0	28	28	172	153	23	3.5	9.2	176	34%	.283
2017	HOU	MLB	34	5	0	0	5	5	34	17	4	1.3	11.4	43	32%	.194
2018	HOU	MLB	35	16	9	0	34	34	214	156	28	1.6	12.2	290	31%	.272
2019	HOU	MLB	36	21	6	0	34	34	223	137	36	1.7	12.1	300	36%	.219
2020	HOU	MLB	37	15	6	0	29	29	184	138	28	2.3	12.1	248	35%	.274

Comparables: Zack Greinke, A.J. Burnett, Aníbal Sánchez

In the same way he will often leave a little something extra for late in the game, Verlander found a little something extra late in his career, winning his first Cy Old, er, Young award since he was a flamethrowing 28-year-old in 2011. It was a year of milestones for the future Hall of Famer, eclipsing 3,000 career strikeouts, registering his first-ever 300-K season, and became just the sixth pitcher in baseball history to throw three no-hitters. Astoundingly, you could argue he has never looked better than he has the past two years. Here's a fact so crazy we had to check three times just to make sure it is true: 21 percent of his career strikeouts have come in an Astros uniform.

YEAR	TEAM	LVL	AGE	WHIP	ERA	DRA	WARP	MPH	FB%	WHF	CSP
2017	DET	MLB	34	1.28	3.82	4.03	3.0	97.7	58	11	47.8
2017	HOU	MLB	34	0.65	1.06	3.08	0.9	97.5	59.6	15.1	49.9
2018	HOU	MLB	35	0.90	2.52	2.33	7.3	97.5	61.2	16.2	51.6
2019	HOU	MLB	36	0.80	2.58	2.51	7.9	96.8	49.9	17.5	48.3
2020	HOU	MLB	37	1.01	2.75	2.95	5.3	95.8	54.6	15.1	48.2

Justin Verlander, continued

Pitch Shape vs LHH

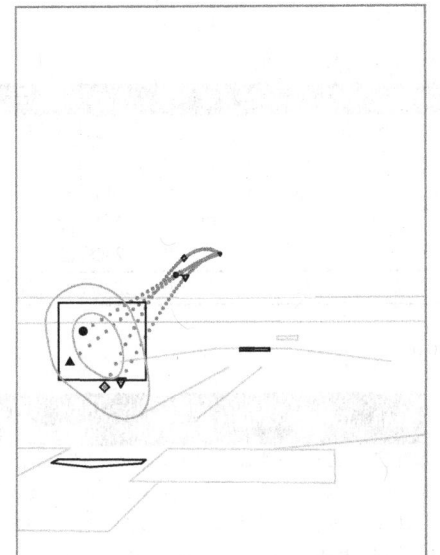

Pitch Shape vs RHH

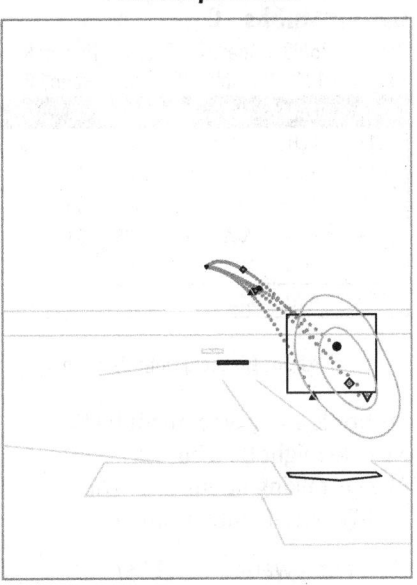

Type	Frequency	Velocity	H Movement	V Movement
● Fastball	49.8%	94.8 [107]	-8.6 [92]	-9.8 [116]
☐ Sinker				
+ Cutter				
▲ Changeup	4.2%	87.2 [107]	-14.2 [86]	-23.7 [111]
✕ Splitter				
▽ Slider	28.7%	87.7 [114]	3.9 [95]	-26.7 [119]
◇ Curveball	17.3%	79.6 [103]	6.9 [98]	-49.8 [95]
⊕ Slow Curveball				
✱ Knuckleball				
▼ Screwball				

PLAYER COMMENTS WITHOUT GRAPHS

Garrett Stubbs C
Born: 05/26/93 Age: 27 Bats: L Throws: R
Height: 5'10" Weight: 175 Origin: Round 8, 2015 Draft (#229 overall)

YEAR	TEAM	LVL	AGE	PA	R	2B	3B	HR	RBI	BB	K	SB	CS	AVG/OBP/SLG
2017	CCH	AA	24	300	36	13	0	4	25	32	44	8	0	.236/.324/.331
2017	FRE	AAA	24	91	11	5	0	0	12	11	15	3	0	.221/.341/.286
2018	FRE	AAA	25	340	60	19	6	4	38	35	53	6	0	.310/.382/.455
2019	ROU	AAA	26	235	33	11	0	7	23	24	38	12	2	.240/.332/.397
2019	HOU	MLB	26	39	8	3	0	0	2	4	7	1	0	.200/.282/.286
2020	HOU	MLB	27	140	14	7	0	3	14	13	26	2	0	.225/.303/.361

Comparables: Joe Ginsberg, John Jaso, Chris Herrmann

Stubbs is a guy who might be fine/
He also might be a bust-a/
Always talking about Triple-A/
And Twenty-Eighteen stats/

No, I don't want no Stubbs/
Stubbs is a guy that can't get no starts from me/
A catcher on the shorter side, with a bat so light/
Trying to holla at me/

YEAR	TEAM	P. COUNT	FRM RUNS	BLK RUNS	THRW RUNS	TOT RUNS
2017	CCH	8443	4.5	2.1	0.5	6.5
2017	FRE	2836	0.3	0.3	-0.1	0.3
2018	FRE	10886	7.8	0.2	1.5	9.5
2019	HOU	1145	-0.5	-0.9	0.0	-1.4
2019	ROU	7765	8.2	0.1	0.6	8.6
2020	HOU	5150	-1.6	-1.6	-0.1	-3.3

YEAR	TEAM	LVL	AGE	PA	DRC+	VORP	BABIP	BRR	FRAA	WARP
2017	CCH	AA	24	300	94	10.9	.269	2.3	C(64): 8.8	2.3
2017	FRE	AAA	24	91	80	1.8	.274	1.9	C(19): 0.5	0.4
2018	FRE	AAA	25	340	116	30.6	.361	3.0	C(75): 10.5, RF(2): -0.2	3.6
2019	ROU	AAA	26	235	85	9.8	.261	0.7	C(54): 8.8, 2B(5): -0.8	1.5
2019	HOU	MLB	26	39	79	0.8	.250	0.2	C(11): -1.5, LF(7): -0.1	-0.1
2020	HOU	MLB	27	140	77	2.3	.258	0.0	C -3	-0.1

Francis Martes RHP

Born: 11/24/95 Age: 24 Bats: R Throws: R
Height: 6'1" Weight: 225 Origin: International Free Agent, 2012

YEAR	TEAM	LVL	AGE	W	L	SV	G	GS	IP	H	HR	BB/9	K/9	K	GB%	BABIP
2017	FRE	AAA	21	0	2	0	8	8	32^1	40	5	7.8	10.6	38	39%	.380
2017	HOU	MLB	21	5	2	0	32	4	54^1	51	7	5.1	11.4	69	44%	.328
2018	FRE	AAA	22	0	1	0	4	4	18^2	25	2	8.2	7.7	16	40%	.397
2020	HOU	MLB	24	1	1	0	28	0	29	26	5	4.6	10.9	35	40%	.297

Comparables: Tyler Danish, Casey Kelly, Taijuan Walker

It's hard to believe just three years ago Martes was the Astros No. 1 prospect. He toiled in the bullpen in 2017 before losing most of 2018 and 2019 to elbow discomfort as a prerequisite to Tommy John surgery. He's thrown just 25 innings over the last two seasons. Still, he's only 24 years old with the fastball-slider-curveball-changeup mix to be a legitimate starter in the big leagues. The only problem is the Astros might be too good to let him fail as he builds back his strength, relegating him to the bullpen for the time being.

YEAR	TEAM	LVL	AGE	WHIP	ERA	DRA	WARP	MPH	FB%	WHF	CSP
2017	FRE	AAA	21	2.10	5.29	6.61	-0.3				
2017	HOU	MLB	21	1.51	5.80	4.39	0.6	98.3	55.4	13.5	46.7
2018	FRE	AAA	22	2.25	6.75	7.97	-0.5				
2020	HOU	MLB	24	1.41	4.74	4.55	0.2	98.1	57.1	13.9	48.1

Lance McCullers Jr. RHP
Born: 10/02/93 Age: 26 Bats: L Throws: R
Height: 6'1" Weight: 205 Origin: Round 1, 2012 Draft (#41 overall)

YEAR	TEAM	LVL	AGE	W	L	SV	G	GS	IP	H	HR	BB/9	K/9	K	GB%	BABIP
2017	HOU	MLB	23	7	4	0	22	22	118^2	114	8	3.0	10.0	132	62%	.330
2018	HOU	MLB	24	10	6	0	25	22	128^1	100	12	3.5	10.0	142	56%	.278
2020	HOU	MLB	26	9	6	0	41	19	126	118	20	4.2	10.5	147	54%	.305

Comparables: Luis Severino, Alex Reyes, Aaron Sanchez

A quick-Twitch athlete—in that he has raw athleticism and streams himself playing Fortnite—McCullers spent 2019 recovering from Tommy John surgery. His breaking ball, whatever you want to call it, is a performance art piece. Sometimes it's a 12-6 loop, sometimes it's Turn 3 at Daytona. It's so lethal, he doesn't even practice it in his bullpens, choosing to save its magic and his fingernail for when he needs it in a game. It will be interesting to see what fastball he pairs it with, having gone with a four-seam in the past before switching to a two-seam in 2018, though the velocity stayed the same at 93-95. He found a changeup grip he liked from scrolling through the Pitching Ninja's Twitter feed and used it to dominate in 2018, to the tune of a .136 batting average against, even better than his famous curve. He's a rescue animal advocate, a great follow on social media, and a healthy season away from being a household name.

YEAR	TEAM	LVL	AGE	WHIP	ERA	DRA	WARP	MPH	FB%	WHF	CSP
2017	HOU	MLB	23	1.30	4.25	4.13	1.9	96.9	40.4	12.8	45.4
2018	HOU	MLB	24	1.17	3.86	3.30	3.0	96.6	37.4	14.3	43.9
2020	HOU	MLB	26	1.40	4.66	4.47	1.5	96.3	39.3	13.9	45.3

Cionel Pérez LHP

Born: 04/21/96 Age: 24 Bats: L Throws: L
Height: 5'11" Weight: 170 Origin: International Free Agent, 2016

YEAR	TEAM	LVL	AGE	W	L	SV	G	GS	IP	H	HR	BB/9	K/9	K	GB%	BABIP
2017	QUD	A	21	4	3	2	12	9	55^1	52	2	2.8	8.9	55	51%	.331
2017	BCA	A+	21	2	1	0	5	4	25^1	27	1	1.8	6.4	18	46%	.325
2017	CCH	AA	21	0	0	0	4	3	13	15	1	3.5	6.9	10	33%	.341
2018	CCH	AA	22	6	1	1	16	11	68^1	54	3	2.9	10.9	83	47%	.304
2018	HOU	MLB	22	0	0	0	8	0	11^1	6	3	5.6	9.5	12	58%	.130
2019	ROU	AAA	23	2	1	0	13	10	47	53	6	4.6	8.2	43	54%	.343
2019	HOU	MLB	23	1	1	0	5	0	9	11	3	2.0	7.0	7	48%	.286
2020	HOU	MLB	24	1	1	0	11	0	12	13	3	4.8	9.7	13	48%	.334

Comparables: Ranger Suárez, Touki Toussaint, Zack Littell

Look, we're not here to judge, but Pérez's stat line is already trending towards "May Have Peaked At 18" and that mullet/goatee combo isn't exactly helping to dispel that notion. After shredding the Cuban league as a teenager, Pérez has not been able to find that same success in Houston's organization. A forearm injury limited him to 63 2/3 innings in 2019, and they were not particularly exciting ones, either. He threw his slider a tick-and-a-half slower this year, which got him shredded at the big-league level. He's still young. He's still left-handed. He still sits in the mid-90s. But next year is going to tell us a lot about his potential. The Astros chose not to carry a single lefty in their bullpen for most of the year and postseason, which theoretically gives him ample opportunity to prove himself.

YEAR	TEAM	LVL	AGE	WHIP	ERA	DRA	WARP	MPH	FB%	WHF	CSP
2017	QUD	A	21	1.25	4.39	4.34	0.6				
2017	BCA	A+	21	1.26	2.84	4.80	0.1				
2017	CCH	AA	21	1.54	5.54	5.70	-0.1				
2018	CCH	AA	22	1.11	1.98	3.36	1.5				
2018	HOU	MLB	22	1.15	3.97	4.58	0.0	97.3	63.2	11.8	41.6
2019	ROU	AAA	23	1.64	5.36	4.89	0.8				
2019	HOU	MLB	23	1.44	10.00	6.79	-0.1	97.3	61.5	10.6	41.7
2020	HOU	MLB	24	1.67	6.56	5.95	-0.1	97.1	64.2	11.6	42.9

Forrest Whitley RHP

Born: 09/15/97   Age: 22   Bats: R   Throws: R
Height: 6'7"   Weight: 195   Origin: Round 1, 2016 Draft (#17 overall)

YEAR	TEAM	LVL	AGE	W	L	SV	G	GS	IP	H	HR	BB/9	K/9	K	GB%	BABIP
2017	QUD	A	19	2	3	0	12	10	46^1	42	2	4.1	13.0	67	37%	.388
2017	BCA	A+	19	3	1	0	7	6	31^1	28	2	2.6	14.4	50	40%	.394
2017	CCH	AA	19	0	0	0	4	2	14^2	8	1	2.5	16.0	26	48%	.292
2018	CCH	AA	20	0	2	0	8	8	26^1	15	2	3.8	11.6	34	39%	.220
2019	BCA	A+	21	1	0	0	2	2	8^1	4	0	1.1	11.9	11	44%	.222
2019	CCH	AA	21	2	2	0	6	6	22^2	18	2	7.5	14.3	36	47%	.372
2019	ROU	AAA	21	0	3	0	8	5	24^1	35	9	5.5	10.7	29	32%	.394
2020	HOU	MLB	22	2	2	0	33	0	35	36	6	4.0	10.9	42	38%	.332

Comparables: Lucas Sims, Clayton Kershaw, Alex Reyes

This Forrest is getting dangerously close to becoming a MarkAppelago. The list of successful, much less impactful, big leaguers with ERAs hovering around 8 for an entire season in the minors is not very long. But Whitley's arsenal is just too good to not find success eventually...right? He led the Arizona Fall League in strikeouts for the second straight year and despite getting knocked around, he had double-digit strikeout rates in every uniform he put on (five teams from levels spanning Rookie Ball to Triple-A).

YEAR	TEAM	LVL	AGE	WHIP	ERA	DRA	WARP	MPH	FB%	WHF	CSP
2017	QUD	A	19	1.36	2.91	3.98	0.7				
2017	BCA	A+	19	1.18	3.16	3.17	0.8				
2017	CCH	AA	19	0.82	1.84	2.28	0.5				
2018	CCH	AA	20	0.99	3.76	2.29	0.9				
2019	BCA	A+	21	0.60	2.16	2.27	0.3				
2019	CCH	AA	21	1.63	5.56	5.46	-0.1				
2019	ROU	AAA	21	2.05	12.21	7.64	-0.2				
2020	HOU	MLB	22	1.46	5.12	4.96	0.1				

LINEOUTS

Hitters

HITTER	POS	TEAM	LVL	AGE	PA	R	2B	3B	HR	RBI	BB	K	SB	CS	AVG/OBP/SLG	DRC+	WARP
Ross Adolph	OF	QUD	A	22	288	45	15	5	6	24	37	99	9	8	.223/.354/.403	114	1.4
	OF	BCA	A+	22	172	24	5	1	1	16	24	43	2	1	.236/.360/.306	112	0.6
Colin Barber	CF	AST	Rk	18	119	19	5	1	2	6	19	29	2	1	.263/.387/.394	139	0.0
Jordan Brewer	OF	TCV	A-	21	56	5	0	0	1	3	2	6	2	0	.130/.161/.185	31	-0.3
Ronnie Dawson	OF	ROU	AAA	24	39	1	1	0	0	3	3	11	1	0	.147/.231/.176	26	-0.2
	OF	CCH	AA	24	459	71	20	2	17	50	47	141	13	10	.212/.320/.403	98	1.3
Taylor Jones	1B	ROU	AAA	25	531	86	28	0	22	84	68	112	0	1	.291/.388/.501	123	2.9
Grae Kessinger	INF	QUD	A	21	201	25	6	0	2	17	26	32	8	2	.224/.333/.294	105	0.8
	INF	TCV	A-	21	45	5	4	0	0	3	3	4	1	1	.268/.333/.366	136	0.4
Korey Lee	C	TCV	A-	20	259	31	6	4	3	28	28	49	8	5	.268/.359/.371	140	1.8
J.J. Matijevic	OF	CCH	AA	23	312	41	21	1	9	35	27	97	8	0	.246/.314/.423	107	1.2
Freudis Nova	INF	QUD	A	19	299	35	20	1	3	29	15	68	10	7	.259/.301/.369	105	0.8
Jeremy Pena	SS	QUD	A	21	289	44	8	4	5	41	35	57	17	6	.293/.389/.421	154	2.9
	SS	BCA	A+	21	185	28	13	3	2	13	12	33	3	4	.317/.378/.467	144	1.7
Luis Santana	SS	CCH	AA	19	66	5	2	0	0	2	6	9	0	0	.228/.333/.263	93	-0.1
	SS	TCV	A-	19	186	19	8	0	2	15	14	24	4	2	.267/.339/.352	139	0.9

Acquired in the J.D. Davis trade, **Ross Adolph** walked half as often as he struck out this year, which isn't bad until you realize he struck out 142 times. ⓧ Comb through his resume, and you'll see **Collin Barber** got a million dollars as a fourth-round pick out of high school. He keeps his hands high and tight which leads to a cut that buzzes through the strike zone. ⓧ Recruited by major programs as a wide receiver, **Jordan Brewer** couldn't catch a break in his first stint in pro ball. ⓧ A tantalizing tools-heavy prospect, **Ronnie Dawson** struggled mightily in the upper levels of the minors, striking out almost a third of the time. ⓧ **Taylor Jones** is 6-foot-7, went to Gonzaga and managed not to play basketball, instead opting to pitch and play first base. After refining his strike zone defense at the plate in 2019, he could see the majors in 2020. ⓧ A second-round pick with a first-round name, **Graeber Crawley Kessinger** wasn't known for his bat until he broke out as a junior at Ole Miss. It hasn't translated to pro ball yet, but there's a lot of potential in his 6'2" frame. ⓧ With an above-average arm and a huge junior season at Cal, **Korey Lee** came off the board earlier than some expected. With no one blocking him in the system and a solid pro debut, he could arrive in the majors quickly. ⓧ A former Cape Cod League darling, **J.J. Matijevic** missed 50 games after a suspension, then struck out almost 10 times for every home run he hit in 2019. It's not what you want. ⓧ He may not stay at shortstop, but **Freudis Nova** still has all the tools to become a big leaguer. You could look at his 2019 stat line and call him a bust, but that would be psycho analysis. ⓧ His father Geronimo played in the big leagues, which provided **Jeremy Pena** with a solid jumping off point. He looked over-matched in the AFL, but that can't dampen his otherwise stellar first full pro season. ⓧ A stocky second baseman with solid bat-to-ball skills, **Luis Santana** resupplied the #Beef lost when J.D. Davis went to the Mets in the same transaction.

Pitchers

PITCHER	TEAM	LVL	AGE	W	L	SV	G	GS	IP	H	HR	BB/9	K/9	K	GB%	WHIP	ERA	DRA	WARP
Brandon Bielak	CCH	AA	23	3	0	0	8	6	36	29	3	3.5	8.2	33	53%	1.19	3.75	4.03	0.4
	ROU	AAA	23	8	4	0	15	14	85^2	69	10	3.8	9.0	86	44%	1.23	4.41	2.73	3.3
Hunter Brown	TCV	A-	20	2	2	0	12	6	23^2	13	0	6.8	12.5	33	53%	1.31	4.56	3.88	0.3
Humberto Castellanos	QUD	A	21	3	0	4	14	0	36^1	29	4	1.5	11.4	46	47%	0.96	3.22	3.37	0.6
	BCA	A+	21	1	1	3	15	0	25^2	30	1	2.1	9.5	27	64%	1.40	3.16	5.92	-0.4
	ROU	AAA	21	0	1	0	5	0	12^2	4	1	2.1	7.1	10	57%	0.55	1.42	2.52	0.5
Brett Conine	QUD	A	22	3	2	0	6	5	33	19	3	1.6	10.9	40	61%	0.76	1.91	2.78	0.9
	BCA	A+	22	4	2	0	15	8	63^1	52	3	2.4	11.4	80	55%	1.09	2.42	3.62	1.0
	CCH	AA	22	1	0	0	4	2	18	20	1	3.0	7.0	14	53%	1.44	2.00	6.13	-0.3
Cody Deason	QUD	A	22	5	3	0	14	11	60^1	42	3	4.6	11.3	76	41%	1.21	3.28	3.75	1.0
	BCA	A+	22	4	3	1	9	6	40^1	34	0	3.1	9.8	44	50%	1.19	3.57	3.75	0.6
Dean Deetz	ROU	AAA	25	2	0	2	24	0	34	32	8	9.8	13.5	51	41%	2.03	7.15	5.72	0.2
Kent Emanuel	ROU	AAA	27	8	2	1	28	7	101^2	98	9	2.0	7.2	81	57%	1.19	3.90	2.49	3.9
Tyler Ivey	CCH	AA	23	4	0	0	11	8	46	28	5	3.1	11.9	61	39%	0.96	1.57	2.84	1.1
Cristian Javier	BCA	A+	22	2	0	1	7	5	28^2	15	1	5.0	12.6	40	33%	1.08	0.94	2.87	0.7
	CCH	AA	22	6	3	3	17	11	74	31	5	4.7	13.9	114	31%	0.95	2.07	2.11	2.5
	ROU	AAA	22	0	0	0	2	2	11	5	1	3.3	13.1	16	17%	0.82	1.64	2.66	0.4
Enoli Paredes	BCA	A+	23	3	1	0	10	6	44	21	3	4.3	12.1	59	45%	0.95	1.64	2.60	1.2
	CCH	AA	23	2	3	1	12	6	50	29	1	3.8	12.4	69	38%	1.00	3.78	2.86	1.2
Jose Alberto Rivera	QUD	A	22	5	5	1	18	11	75^2	61	2	4.3	11.3	95	44%	1.28	3.81	4.14	0.8
Nivaldo Rodriguez	QUD	A	22	3	1	0	6	6	31	23	2	1.2	11.3	39	0%	0.87	1.16		
	BCA	A+	22	3	5	2	18	9	74	46	5	3.8	9.1	75	0%	1.04	2.92		
Jayson Schroeder	AST	Rk	19	1	0	0	3	1	6^1	3	0	7.1	7.1	5	29%	1.26	0.00	4.97	0.1
	TCV	A-	19	0	4	0	6	4	12^2	19	1	16.3	7.8	11	51%	3.32	8.53		
	QUD	A	19	0	1	0	3	1	6	7	0	13.5	13.5	9	19%	2.67	12.00	7.67	-0.2
Peter Solomon	BCA	A+	22	0	0	0	2	2	7^2	7	1	4.7	16.4	14	33%	1.43	2.35	4.03	0.1
Blake Taylor	SLU	A+	23	2	2	7	21	0	27^1	24	1	4.0	9.5	29	67%	1.32	2.63	4.95	-0.1
	BIN	AA	23	0	1	3	18	0	39	25	2	2.8	10.4	45	53%	0.95	1.85	3.31	0.6

After flying up prospect lists in 2018, **Brandon Bielak** failed to replicate his success last season. It seems his early K/9s were all bark and no bite. ⓧ The star of the reality show *Sister Wives* shares a surname with Houston's latest fifth-round pick, **Hunter Brown**. They both have eye-popping SO (strikeout and significant other) numbers. ⓧ He won't overpower you, but he sure as hell won't walk you either. **Humberto Castellanos** keeps getting dudes out no matter what level you put him at. ⓩ A less-than-stellar ERA his junior year caused **Brett Conine** to slip to the 11th round where the Astros were waiting. He's a breakout star with back-to-back years with double digit strikeout rates. Call him Brett K/9. ⓩ The walks are concerning, but **Cody Deason** posted a double-digit strikeout rate and paired it with mid-3 ERAs across two levels. More like Cody Decent. ⓩ 2019 was a crazy year for **Dean Deetz**. Nuts that he fell off so much, walking almost a batter per inning after a 2018 season that held so much promise. ⓩ It's got to be hard being a low-ceiling pitching prospect in a system like Houston's, as **Kent Emanuel** has spent five years in the upper minors, perfecting his averageness. The reward: He was added to the 40-man roster this winter to protect him from Rule 5. Another five years and he might make the 25-man. ⓩ **Tyler Ivey** doesn't throw particularly hard, but he does fill up the strike zone. So far, that's led to a ton of success. Whether it can be done against big leaguers remains to be seen. ⓩ There's not much left for **Cristian Javier** to prove, having just been named the Astros Minor League Pitcher of the Year with a 1.74 ERA across the top three levels. His fastball sits in the low 90s, but his breaking ball is a thing of beauty. ⓩ You're not going to believe this but the Astros have a pitcher in their system that is getting a ton of strikeouts without walking anyone. **Enoli Paredes** continues to blow through the lower levels. The diminutive righty sits in the mid-90s but it's not hard to imagine him flirting with triple digits out of the 'pen. ⓩ **Jose Alberto Rivera** is from a city in the Dominican Republic called San Cristóbal. He's hovered around a 3.50 ERA at every level of the minor leagues, but it's impossible to tell if that success will continue in the future, sans crystal ball. ⓩ **Nivaldo Rodriguez** has found success at every level by using a low-90s fastball up, and curve and change down. Call it the Paul Giamatti profile: it's not sexy but it works. ⓩ Until you open the box score, you can't know if **Jayson Schroeder**'s prospect status is alive or dead. Once you do, though, you see a young, second-round pick who issued multiple free passes in all but one of his appearances in 2019. ⓩ **Jairo Solis** missed all of last season while recovering from Tommy John surgery, but showed a tantalizing live arm in 2018. ⓩ Drafted in the fourth round out of Notre Dame, **Peter Solomon** has had double digit K/9s at every level. He had Tommy John during the summer. The real story here is his Twitter account consists almost entirely of quotes from *The Office*. Here's one to tryout after his next punchout, "Fool me once, strike one. But fool me twice, strike three." ⓩ The Mets got then-lived armed prep lefty **Blake Taylor** way back in June 2014 for Ike Davis. Taylor's time in the Mets' system outlasted Davis' professional career, but came to an end when he was traded to the Astros for Jake Marisnick in December. He's now a semi-interesting relief prospect.

Astros Prospects

The State of the System
The system has thinned out across the contention cycle, and the 'stros haven't been able to develop the kind of solid major league arms that would keep them from running bullpen games in the playoffs.

The Top Ten

1 ★ ★ ★ *2020 Top 101 Prospect* **#26** ★ ★ ★
Forrest Whitley   RHP   OFP: 70   ETA: 2020
Born: 09/15/97   Age: 22   Bats: R   Throws: R   Height: 6'7"   Weight: 195
Origin: Round 1, 2016 Draft (#17 overall)

The Report: It was yet another abbreviated year for 2016's 17th-overall selection due to shoulder fatigue and mechanical issues. The tall right-hander only managed to hurl 59 2/3 innings across four levels, including four rehab starts, and walked 44 batters in those outings. Even with the setbacks and command issues, Whitley still showed plenty of upside with his 86 combined punchouts. He looked much better during his second consecutive trip to the Arizona Fall League, where he led the league in strikeouts once again, showing off his baffling four-pitch mix.

Whitley's mid-90s fastball features plenty of life, and although he struggles to command it more than the secondaries, it is a plus, swing-and-miss offering. A devastating mid-80s changeup with sink and fade pairs extremely well the fastball, and he's not afraid to throw it to both right- and left-handed batters. He has shown excellent feel and command for the "cambio." Both of Whitley's breaking pitches are swing-and-miss offerings as well. His power slider displays late, sharp horizontal break with plus tilt and can hit 90 mph. A 12-6 low-80s curveball is a wipeout pitch with depth and late bite. With four pitches that he can get strikes with in any count, Whitley has the potential to be a dominant starter.

Variance: Higher than ideal at this stage of his development. Health issues have persisted throughout Whitley's four-year professional career, leaving serious doubts as to whether his body can hold up. He has also battled mechanical issues that still seem to flare up from time-to-time.

Mark Barry's Fantasy Take: The Comp: James Bond, *James Bond Franchise*

Houston Astros 2020

We're starting with the biggest name, and perhaps the most flashy talent. Whitley opened the season as the game's most promising pitching prospect, and managed to get himself into quite the predicament, battling injuries and his mechanics en route to the worst statistical season of his career. Luckily he has plenty of gadgets that can help him succeed in an organization that should be able to maximize his immense talent—by any means necessary. The hurler is a good buy low (or at least lower, he'll likely still be quite highly valued) candidate this offseason, especially if other managers are queasy looking at this season's ratios as the potential for a top-line fantasy starter is still there. The 2019 volatility might have unseated Whitley as the top pitching prospect in baseball, but our collective fantasy confidence in the 22-year-old should be shaken, not stirred (ah well, I tried).

─────── ★ ★ ★ *2020 Top 101 Prospect* **#82** ★ ★ ★ ───────

2
Jose Urquidy   RHP   OFP: 60   ETA: 2019
Born: 05/01/95   Age: 25   Bats: R   Throws: R   Height: 6'0"   Weight: 180
Origin: International Free Agent, 2015

The Report: You're probably already familiar with Urquidy, who pitched one of the best games of the 2019 postseason, five dominant innings in what was supposed to be a bullpen game in Game 4 of the World Series. He throws a solid fastball, sitting in the 92-94 range and touching 96, that he gets the most out of due to plus command. His primary offspeed has typically been a plus changeup, but he started relying on a slider as his out-pitch more and more as the playoffs progressed, and it was flashing huge. You may have seen the GIFs of said slider making batters look completely ridiculous on Twitter. He also mixes in a curveball for a fourth look.

You may be less familiar with his background. It's a bit of an exaggeration to say he came out of nowhere—he came up in research for this list last offseason, although he wasn't close at all to making it, and he was exposed to and went unpicked in the Rule 5 Draft. He was a known prospect, but not a top one, and it was under a different name; he played as Jose Luis Hernandez until this past spring.

Why was Urquidy overlooked for so long? He didn't make his pro debut until he was 20, which is on the old side even as overaged international signings go. Just when he was starting to get going as a prospect, he underwent Tommy John surgery, which wiped out his entire 2017 and the first half of 2018. He's a short right-hander without an electric fastball, which is a demographic that is easy to overlook and tends to end up in relief.

He's not overlooked anymore. He's very likely to start 2020 in Houston's rotation, and could stick there for a long time.

Variance: Medium. Urquidy is obviously already MLB-ready, and threw 154 innings total this year. He's still a short pitcher with a recent Tommy John in his background. There's also positive variance here if the slider goes from "flashing huge" to "consistently huge." We're trying not to overreact too much to what might've just been the game of his life, but everyone saw it…

Mark Barry's Fantasy Take: The Comp: Jason Bourne, *The Bourne Franchise*

As mentioned above, you might recall Urquidy as Jose Luis Hernandez, just like you might remember Bourne as David Webb. Also like Bourne, Urquidy beasted in the World Series, putting a bow on a breakout 2019 campaign. The gaudy minor-league strikeout numbers didn't completely follow Urquidy to Houston, but his swinging-strike rate was better than league average, and most of his near-4.00 ERA came from two rocky outings against the Indians and Angels. I like Urquidy quite a bit, and could see an SP3 upside, with an SP5 floor. He'll be eminently useful in all formats.

★ ★ ★ *2020 Top 101 Prospect* **#100** ★ ★ ★

3 Jeremy Pena SS   OFP: 55   ETA: 2021
Born: 09/22/97   Age: 22   Bats: R   Throws: R   Height: 6'0"   Weight: 179
Origin: Round 3, 2018 Draft (#102 overall)

The Report: No prospect in the Astros' system gained more helium this season than Pena. The former University of Maine star dazzled in the field, showing off one of the top gloves in the organization. An athletic frame, great instincts, and a strong, accurate arm combine to give Pena the tools to not only stick at the six for the foreseeable future, but to develop into an asset there. The offensive strides he made in 2019 really proved a separator for him in the system, however, helping him leapfrog other more-heralded prospects in the organizational food chain. He shows natural bat-to-ball skills and he controlled the zone well in both of his stops at A-ball. The swing is geared mostly for line drives, but the power should develop into something close to fringe-average for a middle infielder. On the bases, Pena is a threat to steal or take an extra base thanks to above-average foot speed and an aggressive nature.

Variance: Medium. One breakout season in the low minors is all Pena has under his belt, and he's yet to face advanced pitching to test out the offensive gains. The glove and speed combination make for a high-floor utility player, though.

Mark Barry's Fantasy Take: The Comp: Philip Jennings, *The Americans*

There are no frills with Jennings, just as there are no frills with Pena. "The glove and speed combination make for a high-floor utility player"—not really the stuff fantasy dreams are made of. Both are better in real life than they are in fantasy. Jennings rose to the occasion when challenged with high-level competition, and Pena should get the opportunity to do just that this season.

Perhaps some of Pena's line drives clear the wall, and perhaps his aggression manifests itself into double-digit steals. Even then, that's not a terribly exciting offensive profile.

4. Abraham Toro 3B

OFP: 55   ETA: 2019
Born: 12/20/96   Age: 23   Bats: B   Throws: R   Height: 6'1"   Weight: 190
Origin: Round 5, 2016 Draft (#157 overall)

The Report: Toro's ascent to the big leagues has bubbled under the surface of the system a bit, but outside of a bumpy Double-A debut a couple years ago he's made steady, consistent progress on his path to the majors. A switch-hitter, his left-handed stroke is the more fluid of the two, featuring good balance, fluidity, and enough plane to lift balls with carry to the pull side. His right-handed stroke gets a little less out of the legs, and he's run into some trouble against high-level pitching from that side, but he still shows solid barrel control and a nice approach. Above-average raw should settle in around average game power, and the hit tool projects similarly.

A former catcher, Toro boasts a carrying tool in his arm, the strength of which helps him cover some for uneven reads and slower actions at the hot corner. He's made progress with his footwork and agility, though, to where an average glove is within reach. It's not an especially sexy profile, as prospect ceilings go, but he's more or less ready now and can evolve quickly into a steady, consistent starting third baseman with the upside of an above-average regular who gets on base, hits for a little pop, and doesn't hurt you on the dirt.

Variance: Medium. He's still young and may struggle to find opportunities to establish himself early in his career, but it's a relatively well-rounded skill set that should ultimately play just fine.

Mark Barry's Fantasy Take: The Comp: Natasha Romanoff, *Marvel Cinematic Universe*

When you're dealing with the Avengers, sometimes it's tough to stand out among the big names and personalities. Similarly, in an organization which recently churned out guys like Bregman, Alvarez, Tucker and Whitley, unheralded guys like Toro fall by the wayside. I'm in on the 22-year-old, whose biggest knock is really just a lack of playing time. I'm encouraged by his ability to functionally play three infield positions, and his plate discipline seems to have translated to the big-league level, albeit in an ultra-small sample. If Toro can find his way onto the field, in this organization or another, I like him as a top 50-75ish dynasty prospect (which might be a little bullish, but whatever). Underappreciated, but gets the job done, just like Black Widow. Let's just hope {redacted for spoilers}.

5. Bryan Abreu RHP

OFP: 55   ETA: 2019
Born: 04/22/97   Age: 23   Bats: R   Throws: R   Height: 6'1"   Weight: 204
Origin: International Free Agent, 2013

The Report: Abreu spent a good part of 2019 before his big-league debut as a starter, making 16 starts out of 23 total appearances. It's a role that doesn't fit him long term though. Abreu's future impact will be as a bullpen arm. His fastball touches 95-96, mixed with a pair of fringier breaking pitches. The slider at 82-85 has a ton of movement, like a frisbee from right to left. He has a couple extra notches on the slider velo too, tuning it up to 87 at times. The curveball is 81-83, but the shape and command are both below average. With better command of the fastball and slider, Abreu presents a reasonable late innings option for the Astros, but lacks the elite fastball velocity and slider command to be the premier pitcher in a bullpen. Even marginal improvement in both can make Abreu a stalwart in bullpens for years to come.

Variance: Medium. The command takes Abreu out of contention as a starter, putting him into the bullpen. As a reliever, the command issues are workable. Right now, it's good enough to maintain the profile of a late innings reliever. However, should it degrade for any reason that would knock Abreu into last man in the pen/fringe major league status.

Mark Barry's Fantasy Take: The Comp: Jack Ryan, *Jack Ryan Universe*

Though Abreu was impressive in his big-league debut, getting a ton of whiffs and a decent amount of grounders, he's still a long-term reliever, and one without the guarantee of high-leverage use. If you play in a league rostering 250+ prospects or leagues that use holds as a stat, that could be useful, but it limits the upside. It's sort of like taking a highly respected, feature-film character once played by Harrison Ford and shifting him to a streaming service while casting Jim Halpert as the lead. Significantly lower upside (fine, so maybe this one is a stretch, but to be fair, I didn't realize how hard it would be to come up with spy comps for everyone on this list when I started).

6. Korey Lee C

OFP: 55　ETA: Late 2021
Born: 07/25/98　Age: 21　Bats: R　Throws: R　Height: 6'2"　Weight: 205
Origin: Round 1, 2019 Draft (#32 overall)

The Report: Lee was one of the biggest benefactors of being Andrew Vaughn's college teammate, as scouts got to see more of him than perhaps they otherwise would've. Regardless, he was one of the most sought after catchers in the draft not named Adley Rutschman, and it became pretty apparent why after watching just a few innings. Lee is a big-bodied catcher with solid all-around potential who lacks a standout tool. It starts with above-average raw power that plays to all fields, and he also exhibited average game power throughout the entire New York-Penn League season. He does a really good job of not expanding the strike zone on offspeed and breaking pitches, thus forcing pitchers to throw strikes to get him out. As a result, he raked against a weak NYPL pitching class all season long. If he continues forcing pitchers to throw strikes, Lee could be a 15-20 homer catcher who gets on base at a 33 percent clip.

Lee complements his intriguing offensive profile with solid defense behind the dish. He has athletic motions for a 6-foot-2 catcher, including a plus arm that nabbed 33 percent of base stealers. There were times where he looked gassed from the long season, but such is the case for many recently-drafted catchers. Nonetheless, if everything comes together, you've got yourself a very solid catcher capable of playing 120 above-average games behind the dish.

Variance: Medium. Catchers who show defensive ability and even a hint of offensive promise usually find their way to the bigs.

Mark Barry's Fantasy Take: The Comp: Harry Hart, *Kingsman Franchise*

Lee had a 1.034 OPS while cloaked in the gentleman's armour in his final season at Cal, earning him a first-round selection. Much like Harry Hart, he's probably better in fantasy than reality. Lee could be a decent starter behind the dish, and in fantasy circles, "decent" in real life probably translates to top-10 in fantasy. I have a lot of trouble relying on the development path of dudes that don the tools of ignorance (and Ben has chronicled catching prospects, like, a lot), but Lee's athleticism leaves me at least a little optimistic. He's a top-200ish guy, but even that feels a little bold for a guy with only Low-A experience.

7. Rogelio Armenteros   RHP   OFP: 50   ETA: 2019
Born: 06/30/94   Age: 26   Bats: R   Throws: R   Height: 6'1"   Weight: 215
Origin: International Free Agent, 2014

The Report: Ah sweet Rogelio. Another year, and you remain in our hearts and on our list. Armenteros did what he does last year, including a representative 18-inning sample in Houston that saw him whiff a batter every frame while staying off barrels at an even more impressive clip. The burly right-hander is an aggressive attacker of the zone in spite of a modest fastball that sits around 92. The pitch plays up on account of his advanced pitchability, however, and both the curve and especially the change work as competent secondaries. He fiddled with a slider down the stretch that could extend his already deep arsenal that much further. He pitches forwards, backwards, and in all directions, and he generally commands well enough to keep hitters appropriately off-balance. There is both present and future big-league staff utility here, with a multi-inning and spot-start role probably best-suited for his particular skill set. A reliable 100 innings of league-average production at controlled cost is a highly valuable commodity in today's game, and Rogelio is capable of performing in that kind of role as soon as next season.

Variance: Relatively low. He's fully cooked and ready to serve big-league hitters.

Mark Barry's Fantasy Take: The Comp: Cassian Andor, *Rogue One*

For Cassian, he's best when he's motivated and focused on a cause. For Armenteros, well, I hope that's what was going on, as he spent parts of three seasons at Triple-A Round Rock with diminishing returns. The profile isn't overly exciting—the upside of a good spot starter isn't really what you're hoping for outside of the deepest of dynasties or AL-only leagues. Toss Andor, er, Armenteros on the watch list and cross your fingers for a spot in the rotation.

8. Freudis Nova SS

OFP: 50 ETA: 2022
Born: 01/12/00 Age: 20 Bats: R Throws: R Height: 6'1" Weight: 180
Origin: International Free Agent, 2016

The Report: Signed for seven figures out of the Dominican Republic in 2016, Nova has yet to make a big splash stateside. The wiry-framed infielder even took a small step back over 75 games with Quad Cities this year. His strengths are clearly his glove and speed. However, he wasn't even the best shortstop on Quad Cities for most of the year. Jeremy Pena manned the six until he got promoted. That forced Nova to third base, a position where he did not look comfortable. When he did get the chance to play short, he flashed impressive range and athletic ability, along with a plus arm.

On the bases he shows slightly better than average quick-twitch motions and gets solid jumps, making him a base stealing threat as he matures. At the dish, Nova is still very inconsistent. He will flash good bat speed, but catching up to even average heaters on the inner-half gives him trouble. Currently, there isn't much, if any, power at his disposal. And there doesn't seem to be much room for growth either.

Variance: High. There is still a lot of offensive development needed for Nova. Between inconsistent bat speed and an ensuing lack of power, it will be an uphill battle to become an even average threat in the box, which keeps a reserve infielder projection on the table.

Mark Barry's Fantasy Take: The Comp: Cody Banks, *Agent Cody Banks*

The youngest super-spy of all time meets the youngest prospect on our list (we're reaching here, I know). It's almost always too early to write off a dude who can't legally drink for another year-plus, but Nova's 2019 production doesn't really inspire a ton of confidence. Let's monitor him for now, and pounce if/when he shows some consistent power or consistent speed or consistent, well, offense.

9. Cristian Javier RHP

OFP: 50 ETA: 2020
Born: 03/26/97 Age: 23 Bats: R Throws: R Height: 6'1" Weight: 204
Origin: International Free Agent, 2015

The Report: Javier is one of the sneakier pop up arms in the Astros system, as he doesn't exactly fit the typical "Astroball" prototype. Javier stands a hair shorter than his listed 6-foot-1 height, but his list weight appears accurate. He has longer legs and levers with a sturdy backside, and he is a good athlete with quality body control.

The righty's velocity sits in the low 90s with plus arm-side life, and at times he will show average command of the offering; it's more of a craft pitch, as opposed to the typical Astros power arm. He has a true plus low-80s curveball with a tight, slurvy shape that boasts plus spin and depth. Javier also mixes in an average-flashing 83-84 mph changeup with good arm speed and some tumble, although it lacks true swing-and-miss fade. You'll occasionally see a mid-80s slider-ish pitch that he seems to have little feel for, as well.

Javier's command of a quality fastball/curve combo with solid pitchability and command should carry him to a 6th starter or low setup role. If he's unable to iron out the changeup consistency he might settle into more of a middle relief role, but an improvement there along with a half a tick in command and he could see himself in the back of an MLB rotation.

Variance: Medium. Javier's advanced feel for fastball/curve combo gives him a major league outcome on the low end, but his ability to refine the changeup and find another improvement to command will be important to his future development.

Mark Barry's Fantasy Take: The Comp: Varys, *Game of Thrones*

Sometimes spies are crafty and unconventional. Take Varys for instance. By looking at him, you wouldn't necessarily think he'd be a master strategist, capable of high-leverage results (something something book and its cover). Same goes for Javier. He's on the small-ish end and doesn't have premium gas in the tank, so it's easy to underestimate him. I'd take a flier on him in AL-onlys and in leagues with 150-200 prospects or so, betting on the come for the changeup.

10 Jairo Solis   RHP   OFP: 50   ETA: 2023
Born: 12/22/99   Age: 20   Bats: R   Throws: R   Height: 6'2"   Weight: 160
Origin: International Free Agent, 2016

The Report: Solis missed the entire 2019 season while recovering from Tommy John surgery. He moves up within the rankings here anyway because the Astros traded or graduated a lot of their depth and we had already built his surgery into last year's ranking. Going back to 2018 looks, he had the foundations of a three-pitch starting pitcher's arsenal with an above-average fastball supplemented by the makings of a plus curve and average-to-above-average change. The lost year of development time isn't great, but it's not a killer, as Solis had already pitched well in full-season ball at 18. He will pitch the entire 2020 season at 20, so there's plenty of time. We need to see him back on a mound before we get too excited, and he needs to hold up under a starting workload (he was handled very lightly in 2018 and still blew out), but there's a real chance to shoot up the list next year.

Variance: High. He's a young pitcher who just missed an entire year and could be nearly anything.

Mark Barry's Fantasy Take: The Comp: Bran Stark, *Game of Thrones*

No spoilers here, but let's not forget that he took Season 5 off before downloading the entire history of the world through the Weirwood trees and changing the course of Westerosi history. Of course, you have to ignore the whole "he can't walk" thing, as Solis proved plenty capable of that in his 2018 campaign. He's an interesting flier to keep your eye on, just like the Three-Eyed Raven.

The Next Ten

11 **Myles Straw   SS/CF**
Born: 10/17/94   Age: 25   Bats: R   Throws: R   Height: 5'10"   Weight: 180
Origin: Round 12, 2015 Draft (#349 overall)

Straw was a pain in the ass for opposing pitchers in his first Showtime look last season. He rarely swung, forcing an obscene number of pitches in his plate appearances, and then when he finally did offer he flashed elite contact skills in and out of the zone. That tracks with a career-long profile now, as Straw has steadily progressed through the minors on the back of a successful execution of that exact offensive strategy. There is absolutely no power whatsoever, though, and that limits the overall ceiling here. But added defensive versatility, including wholly competent play at the six, pairs intriguingly with on-base skills and elite 80-grade speed that has shown no signs of slipping. He's a fun and valuable player for the depth chart, and there's enough in the raw tools that he can provide average value with a little luck and enough opportunity.

12 **Brandon Bielak   RHP**
Born: 04/02/96   Age: 24   Bats: L   Throws: R   Height: 6'1"   Weight: 210
Origin: Round 11, 2017 Draft (#331 overall)

Bielak is one of my favorite "under the radar" arms due to his impressive four-pitch mix. He throws from the right side as he sits 92-94 with a four-seam fastball that tends to be a bit flat. His primary secondary is a true plus curveball in the upper 70s with plus depth and spin. He mixes in a harder mid-80s, above-average slider with more horizontal shape and above-average break. His mid-80s changeup has the makings of an average pitch with good deception and some tumble, but his command of it comes and goes.

Bielak is comfortable throwing any of his offerings in any count, which makes him fun to watch when he's able to command his fastball. Pitchability is a utilized strength for Bielak and if he's able to limit his main flaw, it could carry him well-beyond his current projection as a 6th starter. His fastball command wobbles, which combined with it being generally a hittable pitch creates significant reliance on his secondaries. If he can find a way to bump the fastball command high enough to allow his secondaries to mix more effectively, Bielak could find himself as a No. 5 starter in a major league rotation.

Houston Astros 2020

13 **Jordan Brewer   OF**
Born: 08/01/97   Age: 22   Bats: R   Throws: R   Height: 6'1"   Weight: 195
Origin: Round 3, 2019 Draft (#106 overall)

A wide receiver recruit out of high school who went from Indiana JuCo to Michigan for his junior year, Brewer has premium athleticism you don't normally find in a third-round college pick, but it's paired with fairly raw present baseball skills. As you'd expect given the background, Brewer is a plus runner with explosive burst. There's plus raw power potential—he's built like a D1 slot receiver—although the loft and plane is inconsistent and he can get long while trying to tap into it. He has enough arm for all three outfield spots, but should stick in center field with more reps. Brewer dealt with turf toe towards the end of the college season, and had a poor and abbreviated pro debut, and there are wildly variant opinions on important topics like "will he actually hit at all?" He's a bit of a mystery box going forward, but the positive variance would be exciting. The progress to any sort of a major league role is more sous vide than flash fry, though.

14 **Garrett Stubbs   C**
Born: 05/26/93   Age: 27   Bats: L   Throws: R   Height: 5'10"   Weight: 175
Origin: Round 8, 2015 Draft (#229 overall)

Stubbs is getting a little long in the tooth for a list like this, but he found his way into a big-league uniform last year and should see more opportunities in the year ahead. We've long been fans of his athleticism, if wary of his frame and lack of pop, and those all remain defining pieces of the puzzle. He moves extremely well behind the dish, with a fluid blocking technique and quick pop that helps his arm play above-average. After years of speculation, Houston did indeed begin to deploy him for game reps at second and in left field last season, and adding that positional versatility should help his chances of sticking for stretches on a 25-man roster. He's a disciplined hitter with solid bat-to-ball skills, but the lack of power has become a problem at higher levels, as pitchers have attacked him at will in the zone to generate favorable counts. Still, he has continued to get on base at a solid clip at just about every turn, and if that holds along with his newfound defensive utility he'll be able to carve out a nice, long career for himself as a valuable bench piece and second-division starter.

15 **Tyler Ivey   RHP**
Born: 05/12/96   Age: 24   Bats: R   Throws: R   Height: 6'4"   Weight: 195
Origin: Round 3, 2017 Draft (#91 overall)

Ivey is an athletic, high-effort mess of a 6-foot-4 right-handed pitcher with wild limbs and jerky movements. Despite that description, he actually has a lot more control of his body during the delivery than you'd expect. Ivey works between 92-95 with his four-seam fastball. The pitch shows plus life and sets up his hard upper-80s slider. That pitch shows plus horizontal break and hard dive when he's on top of it and down in the zone. Ivey's low-80s 11-5 curveball flashes plus with above-average depth. A fringy mid-80s changeup rounds out the repertoire. He maintains his arm speed well on the change, but it remains fairly lifeless through the zone. Ivey has present fringy command, which actually suggests truly impressive body control given his loud delivery, but that delivery does make it hard to project further refinement.

The arsenal is ideal for a low setup role where he can unleash a potent three-pitch mix in short bursts to buzzsaw through a tough group of righties. There's potential rotation upside here if he can somehow manage to add an improved changeup, but he hasn't yet shown it.

16 Grae Kessinger SS
Born: 08/25/97 Age: 22 Bats: R Throws: R Height: 6'2" Weight: 200
Origin: Round 2, 2019 Draft (#68 overall)

The grandson of former Cubs' great, Don Kessinger, Grae shot up draft boards last year after putting together a breakout offensive season at Ole Miss. There were some struggles in his first taste of professional ball which could easily be attributed to fatigue after a deep run in the college playoffs. Expect the bat to eventually play close to average. He has a patient approach and knows the strike zone. The swing is compact and quick, geared toward line drives, but he's athletic enough to develop some pop down the road. Defensively, he's serviceable at short in a pinch but is likely to eventually find a home elsewhere in the infield. None of the tools are loud, but it's a profile that should move quickly through the system and could eventually find its way onto a big league roster.

17 Jose Alberto Rivera RHP
Born: 02/14/97 Age: 23 Bats: R Throws: R Height: 6'3" Weight: 160
Origin: International Free Agent, 2016

Rivera was an overaged signee in 2016 and his pro debut came in the Dominican complex at age 20. This is exactly the kind of prospect who might get squeezed out of organizations under the proposed minor league reshuffling, and that would be a shame. Not every arm develops at the same pace, and yes, Rivera is 22 and in the Midwest League. But fastball don't lie, and Rivera's stuff could get him to the majors quickly. He pumps 95 mph heaters and has two usable secondaries in a diving changeup and big breaking slider with 11-6 depth. The command profile is still rough given his paucity of pro reps, but if the Astros iron that out he could be a useful Swiss-Army-type arm on a modern pitching staff.

18 Luis Santana INF
Born: 07/20/99 Age: 20 Bats: R Throws: R Height: 5'8" Weight: 175
Origin: International Free Agent, 2016

After coming over to Houston as part of the trade that sent J.D. Davis to the Mets, the 5'8" second baseman got an aggressive May fill-in assignment in Double-A before the New York-Penn League season began. Santana was only somewhat overmatched in Double-A, instead of completely so, because of his plus bat-to-ball skills and knowledge of the zone. He starts open and crouched, utilizing a moderate leg kick to effectively time his swings, though sometimes his hands start moving towards the ball before the hips and torso do, leading to occasional weak contact. At his best, Santana effectively uses his stocky frame to help drive balls to the pull-side gap. Yet despite his mature frame, he is not a power hitter, and he will have to spray the ball more if he's to be a successful gap hitter in the bigs. As an average runner and defender at second, Santana doesn't fit your prototypical utilityman mold, but he may hit enough where it doesn't matter. If the hit tool continues to develop and he maintains the weight, I get lots of right-handed Luis Arraez vibes here.

19 Ronnie Dawson OF
Born: 05/19/95 Age: 25 Bats: L Throws: R Height: 6'2" Weight: 225
Origin: Round 2, 2016 Draft (#61 overall)

Dawson has an ideal athlete's build at 6-foot-1, 230 pounds of pure athletic muscle. He has a strong lower half and impressively-built torso and arms. No mere strongman, Dawson is also a good athlete with some quick-twitch and body control. Unfortunately, his offensive profile was almost exactly the kind of profile that tends to over-promise and under-deliver.

Dawson generates plus bat speed and has some barrel control, which leads to a lot of good-quality contact when he gets a hold of a ball. He sees fastball, he hits fastball, for a hard line drive or deep fly ball. He has plus raw power and he swings like it, so he can hit some truly majestic dingers. However, Dawson struggles to recognize breaking balls or offspeed of any kind and regularly misdiagnoses before taking a strong hack at a pitch out of the zone. That's not to say he's overly aggressive, as he actually will lay off pitches he does read, but that doesn't happen enough to make the overall offensive profile play in a corner.

Dawson's an average defender in right despite some inconsistent jumps and routes due to good closing speed and a plus arm. Despite the loud physical tools and a decent defensive profile, Dawson looks to be a better bet to bust than boom. Without marginal improvement with pitch recognition he's unlikely to have much of a major league career and only with significant improvement will be able to settle into a regular role.

20 J.J. Matijevic 1B
Born: 11/14/95 Age: 24 Bats: L Throws: R Height: 6'0" Weight: 206
Origin: Round 2, 2017 Draft (#75 overall)

Previously an outfielder, Matijevic started primarily playing first base this year after his promotion to Double-A, and played it nearly exclusively during the Fall League. He was always headed in that direction, dating back to when he was drafted in 2017 as one of the picks the Astros recouped from the Cardinals as a result of the Chris Correa hacking scandal. His defense in the outfield was rough, and he's still not all the way there at first base yet, but it's a better fit for him moving forward defensively with a maxed out frame. What is still to be determined is whether his bat is a fit at first; he possesses plus raw power that he hasn't yet gotten fully into games, and the swing is on the stiff and pull-happy side. He hits the ball hard and has an idea at the plate, so he's interesting, but the offensive bar at first base is high.

Personal Cheeseball

PC   **Ross Adolph   OF**
Born: 12/17/96   Age: 23   Bats: L   Throws: R   Height: 6'1"   Weight: 203
Origin: Round 12, 2018 Draft (#350 overall)

The other piece of the J.D. Davis deal, Adolph had a weird and uneven season. Part of that was due to being banged up early, but the outfielder warmed up with the temperature in Quad Cities and managed to get a promotion to High-A before the end of the season. Honestly, I expected him to do better as a polished college bat in A-ball, even a Day Three for-slot one, but he struggled with spin from full-season arms, and despite an overall strong approach, chased a bit too much. There's still interesting tools here—sneaky solid raw and a potential above-average glove in center most noteworthy among them—but until Adolph shows he can consistently hit full-season arms, the major league fourth outfielder projection is a lot murkier than it was this time last year.

Low Minors Sleeper

LMS   **Blair Henley   RHP**
Born: 05/14/97   Age: 23   Bats: R   Throws: R   Height: 6'3"   Weight: 190
Origin: Round 7, 2019 Draft (#226 overall)

Drafted but unsigned by the Yankees in 2016, Henley first gained national recognition when he threw three consecutive no-hitters in high school. Henley then attended the University of Texas where he became a respectable starter for the Longhorns en route to being drafted by Houston in the seventh round this past summer. Standing at 6-foot-3, Henley is a lanky, athletic righty with a three-quarters arm slot, who throws enough strikes and utilizes a somewhat funky delivery that can make for an uncomfortable at-bat for fellow righties.

The fastball comes in at 89-93, though it has nice rising action and generates its fair share of swings and misses high in the zone. What makes Henley especially interesting, however, is a plus curveball that displays really nice 11-5 tilt. He can manipulate the pitch inside and outside the zone rather well, and it was consequently one of the best individual pitches in the Penn League this Summer. The change is fringe-average as of now, but he has time to either work on it or experiment with other pitches. The curveball alone will allow him to move up in the minor league ranks, but pair that with his athleticism, a workable heater and solid strike-throwing ability, and he makes for a fun project in an organization which is arguably the best at developing this kind of talent.

Top Talents 25 and Under (as of 4/1/2020)

1. Carlos Correa
2. Yordan Alvarez
3. Forrest Whitley
4. Roberto Osuna
5. Kyle Tucker
6. Jose Urquidy
7. Jeremy Pena
8. Abraham Toro
9. Bryan Abreu
10. Korey Lee

The cutoff for the 25 and Under list is April 1. Alex Bregman, an MVP finalist after finishing with the fourth-highest DRC+ (157) in baseball, turns 26 on March 30. So he is not eligible, but he is there in spirit. Meanwhile, the owner of MLB's seventh-highest DRC+ (Yordan Alvarez, 149) doesn't even top the Astros list.

Houston, like the rest of us, keeps getting older. George Springer and Jose Altuve, both entering their age-30 seasons, are no longer the youthful stars they once were. But the Astros are still loaded with young talent. Correa is a generational star whose only knock has been durability. When he is healthy, there are only a handful of players in the same tier as him. Since his debut in 2015, Correa has a 123 DRC+, the best among all shortstops during that time and a full six points above second place Francisco Lindor.

Alvarez had what the kids are calling, "a year." In 143 combined games between Triple-A and the majors, he hit 50 home runs and drove in 149. His complete lack of defensive value limits his ultimate ceiling, but he's a better baserunner than his frame would lead you to believe and his offensive performance looks as predictable as any other player's, which is to say, who even knows, man.

Tucker and Urquidy will certainly see their roles expand in the 2020 season after shorts stints of varying success levels in 2019. Tucker feasted on fastballs to the tune of a .418 wOBA, but has still shown vulnerability to offspeed stuff, especially backfoot breaking balls from righties. Urquidy blew well past his innings limit but was exactly what the Astros needed with the implosion of Wade Miley down the stretch.

Toro helped Justin Verlander throw a no-hitter with a t-shirt to commemorate the moment and Abreu was as magical as anyone can be in 8 2/3 innings. Pena, as you just read, had a phenomenal year showcasing his glove and his bat. Second, short, and third certainly seem blocked in Houston, but Jack Mayfield appeared in 26 games this year, so anything can happen. The Astros have leapfrogged between short-term catching options ever since Jason Castro left in 2016, so Lee will get his chance to stick soon.

There isn't a ton potential to dream on down the road, but with a championship window wide open right now, having this much young talent ready to contribute at the major leagues is never a bad thing.

Part 3: Featured Articles

The Baseball Is Juiced (Again)

Robert Arthur

This article originally appeared at Baseball Prospectus on April 5, 2019.

It started when the normally reliable Chris Sale got lit up for three homers by the Mariners in the Red Sox's season opener. It was part of a record number of taters that flew on Opening Day, as starters from Sale to Zack Greinke were taken deep by the handful. Then Christian Yelich hit a home run in each of his first four games, tying yet another MLB record, this one for consecutive games with a dinger to start a season.

It didn't take long for fans and players to begin whispering and tweeting about the baseballs being juiced again. It's early yet for us to come to any definitive conclusion about the 2019 season, but preliminary data shows that the baseball has returned to its aerodynamic peak. Whether that means this season will smash home run records like 2017 did remains to be seen.

Before home run explosion over the last few years, no one worried too much about the baseball's air resistance. While MLB and Rawlings (the company that manufactures the official baseballs) kept track of dozens of metrics to make sure that the ball was consistent from month to month, they didn't measure drag.

But drag is incredibly important in determining how likely a hitter is to knock one out of the park. As baseballs become more aerodynamic, they travel further given a certain initial velocity. A deep fly ball that might have been caught at the warning track can instead go into the first row of the stands. A three percent change in drag coefficient can work to add about five feet to a well-hit fly ball, which can in turn increase home runs league wide by an astounding 10-15 percent.

It's possible to measure the aerodynamics of the baseball using the pitch-tracking radars currently in place in each MLB ballpark. By calculating the loss of speed from when the pitch is released to when it crosses the plate, you can directly measure the drag coefficient on the baseball. I first wrote about the role of decreasing drag in boosting home runs in 2017, and MLB's commission of scientists and statisticians later confirmed that the more aerodynamic baseballs in use that year were largely to blame for the spike in home runs. The same commission rejected some alternate hypotheses, like rising temperatures and a league-wide boost in launch angle pushing more balls over the fence.

The current era has featured some large fluctuations in drag coefficient, leading to first an explosion in 2016 and 2017, and then a dialing back of homers last year. Curious about the record-breaking home run tallies in the last few days, I used the same methodology to measure the aerodynamics of the baseballs so far in 2019.

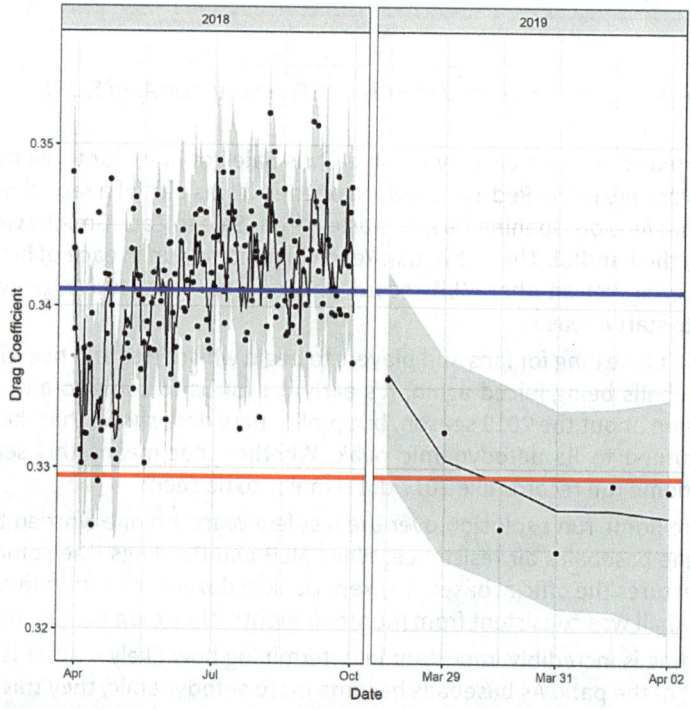

We're only a week into the 2019 season, but the drag numbers so far are among the lowest recorded in the last calendar year. With apologies for gory math, the current 2019 season average drag coefficient (the red line) would be below the 95 percent credible interval (the shaded area) for about nine-tenths of the 2018 season. (I used a Bayesian Random Walk model implemented in INLA to calculate these credible intervals, averaging the drag numbers in each game and adjusting for park.)

There were only a handful of six-day stretches in 2018 that had drag numbers below what we're seeing now, and most were in late June and early July. All of this means that 2019's data so far is quite a bit different than what we saw through most of last year.

These drag coefficients factor out the effects of temperature and air density, so they aren't a product of April cold. However, the numbers could be deceptive if the radars used to track pitches have changed from year to year. I consulted with some experts within baseball who were not aware of any specific modifications to the radar this year that could produce this pattern, but it's an important caveat of which to be aware.

On the one hand, it's only been six days, and we don't quite have the statistical basis to say that these drag coefficients are unprecedented compared to 2018. On the other hand, we've witnessed about 5,000 fastballs so far this season, so it's not as if our sample size is small. At least so far, the baseball has played like it's much more aerodynamic than it was last year. In fact, the current drag coefficient is really only comparable to 2017, when the baseballs were more aerodynamic than they had been in at least a decade.

It's not just fancy radar tracking indicating that the baseball is flying through the air more easily. The current number of home runs per game (as of this writing) is the highest it's been since the heady days of 2017, the year that teams and players broke dinger-related records everywhere you looked. That's especially remarkable considering that we're in what is typically the coldest part of the regular season, when lower temperatures and higher winds tend to suppress offense and keep balls in the air within the park. Comparing only from April to April, this year's rate of home runs per fly ball is even a little bit higher than it was in 2017.

With that said, the current measurements are no guarantee that 2019 will be another year of record-shattering homer hitting. The trouble with the drag measurements is that they are not consistent from June to August, from week to week, or even sometimes from day to day. Whether because of natural manufacturing variation or differences in the underlying supplies of cowhide and thread that go into the baseballs, drag has a tendency to fluctuate up and down over the course of a year. So the homers that fly in the first week of April wouldn't necessarily clear the fence a week later.

It's possible that this one-week drop in drag coefficient subsides and the baseball returns to its 2018 levels. On the other hand, it's almost equally probable that the ball becomes even more slippery and flies ever farther. Either way, it's clear that the baseball's air resistance is something to keep an eye on for the remainder of the 2019 season.

—*Robert Arthur is an author of Baseball Prospectus.*

The Moral Hazard of Playing It Safe

Craig Goldstein

This article originally appeared at Baseball Prospectus on August 6, 2019.

A couple days prior to the trade deadline, amidst a sea of tranquility posing as the lead up to the trade deadline, Bob Nightengale took to Twitter. Nightengale, who was probably wearing his pants backwards at the time, tweeted that MLB GMs were coming around on the idea that the unified trade deadline should be moved back from July 31 to August 15, so they could better assess their positions in the standings and whether they should buy or sell. To which I said:

This might strike some as reductive and churlish. And it might be that, but it isn't really wrong, either. Jeff Quinton wrote a great piece discussing the environmental factors that enable front offices to avoid risk without upsetting the apple cart within their own fanbases. I don't believe that it goes far enough, however. His article gives us the proper framework through which to understand why these behaviors have been allowed to seep into front offices throughout the league. Understanding the reasons behind these actions are different from excusing them, though, and GMs should not be let off the hook for their non-competitive approach to the trade deadline (much less the offseason).

⚾   ⚾   ⚾

It's fair to say that fans as a group have rarely, if ever, been pro-player. It is also fair to say that in the time during and following the Moneyball revolution, the pendulum swung from fans who cared intensely about winning in the moment (and thus might be intolerant of a rebuilding approach) to fans who supported building a team that could compete throughout multiple seasons, viewing the playoffs as a crapshoot, with the thought that getting multiple bites at the apple was a better approach than taking a bigger bite in any one season.

There's nothing wrong with that approach, and I still find merit in that argument. However, it seems that the pendulum has swung too far in that direction. Teams are overvaluing some of the individual factors that make themselves long-term contenders rather than attempting to seize a championship when given the opportunity. It's a difficult needle to thread.

And surely, they (and those in similar positions) would have liked another two weeks to clarify where they stand so as to better marshal their resources. We've all asked for a few more minutes when staring at a menu. But all of these GMs and front office personnel are where they are to make difficult decisions. They have proprietary data and internal analysts dedicated to understanding their position relative to the rest of the league, and how any move in the here and now impacts their long-term vision. To complain (if that report is accurate) that over half the season is not enough to properly assess their season is bullshit of the highest order. Move the deadline, and you'd simply have increasingly discounted trade offers because teams would be acquiring even less control of anyone they're acquiring, rental or not.

Major league front offices are behaving like the managers they lampooned two decades ago. They're effectively sacrificing a runner to second in the ninth inning—not because it's the correct move, but rather because it is safe. It used to be that the phrase "moral hazard" was used to describe general managers who made ill-fated, short-sighted decisions aimed at locking in wins and securing their jobs at the expense of their team's future. Now, general managers are guilty of committing moral hazards in the opposite direction, playing it utterly safe and terrified of becoming scapegoats.

In lieu of bold action, they opt to pussyfoot around a current window of contention, choosing instead to play the long game and stack up years of control like they're blocks in a game of Jenga. GMs pass on signing quality players in free agency because the back-end of the deal might look bad, and because they might be able to squeeze out 70 percent of the production from a player who costs a tenth as much. That's a safer investment, too, because it's also hard to prove a negative—it's impossible to prove that Manny Machado would make the Mets a playoff team in 2019-2020, but it's easy to say that the back half of Robinson Cano's contract sucks. Owners, who rule over GM's jobs, are also humans with human brain processes that will always make the so-called albatross contract uglier than the road not taken.

These days, GMs are remembered for the bad deals they make and the surplus value they generate, not the acquisition of expensive, necessary talents that meet their market worth (or fall slightly short while still providing significant on-field value). And front offices know that one or two expensive misfires can cost them their jobs, no matter how many good deals they make.

No front office exemplifies this ethos more than the Toronto Blue Jays. General Manager Ross Atkins had this to say following the Blue Jays underwhelming trade deadline:

This is by no means the first time that an executive will cite years of control to justify their actions, which is often just another way of saying "don't look at what we got, look at how much we got of it." Atkins touts quantity to elide the discussion of quality—either, that of the players acquired, or those given up. Remember: the other teams presumably value years of control, too.

Atkins also had some thoughts to offer regarding free agents back in early 2018:

This ignores, of course, whether the player can create enough value in the front end of a contract to justify the longer term of a deal, and the decline that often occurs in the back end. It also ignores whether the player can fill a need the team requires and put them in a position to compete for and win a championship. But as teams seemingly avoid contention at all, where they might end up having to consider and later justify some of these tough decisions, we still see risk-averse approaches.

Anthony Fenech's article on two trades that recently extended GM Al Avila didn't make got at this issue rather well:

> Passing on those deals was defensible: Both players had yet to break out and trading [Michael] Fulmer—a pitcher who appeared to be a future ace, no matter his injury concerns—would have taken serious gumption, opening Avila up to strong criticism.

Avoiding strong criticism is something each of us can understand as a motivation, but the avoidance of criticism only matters if that criticism is valid. In Fulmer's case, shoving his injury concerns aside affects not only the years that the team controls him (he is currently missing a full season due to Tommy John surgery) but also the quality of those seasons, as his knee and elbow injuries combined to dampen his effectiveness even when healthy enough to pitch. But it was easy to present the then-current image of Fulmer as a top of the rotation pitcher who the team had under its domain for the next five seasons as something to build around. The status quo isn't nearly as often second-guessed as a decision that disrupts it.

⚾ ⚾ ⚾

MLB GMs are risk-averse to a fault. They are ivy-educated and consulting firm-approved, and yet they can't seem to avoid leaving wins on the table in their all-consuming lust for a non-existent $/WAR championship. They are supposed to zig when everyone else zags, and not merely pay lip service to the idea of zigging through a calculated PR plan built on convincing the fan base their approach is novel when it actually apes most of their competitors. Instead they've become far more concerned with making safe, accepted-by-the-new-common-wisdom decisions, such that our prior understanding of what a moral hazard is has become inverted.

I can't blame them entirely, and not only because of the reasons that Quinton illuminated in his article, but also because of the damage wrought by the introduction of the second wild card (WC2) spot. MLB's desire to have more teams in playoff contention has sparked anti-competitive behavior. Teams know now that they do not need to swing big as they assemble their roster because there is a good chance that a mediocre team can either catch fire and capture a division, or muddle along until they back into the WC2.

Simultaneously, the one-game playoff has neutered the WC1, putting an entire season on the flip of a coin like some sort of baseball-obsessed Anton Chigurh. While the one-game playoff makes sense as a way to increase the value of winning a division, it also means that if a front office doesn't like its chances of overcoming a behemoth like the Dodgers or Astros in the offseason, they have few incentives to chase glory. Similarly, the relative inaction in the NL Central at the trade deadline—despite a wide open division—can be explained by the idea that any high-variance investment could still result in only a wild card (or worse) result, given the mere two months left in the season to make an impact.

⚾ ⚾ ⚾

As stated at the top, we should not confuse reasons for excuses. The implementation of the second wild card is just one of many environmental factors that influence how each front office operates. I am convinced that it is one of the larger factors, but I am also convinced that organizations need to shed the yoke of "efficiency at all costs" so that they can instead pursue competition, as the spirit of the game intends. Until they do, we're all deadline losers.

—*Craig Goldstein is an author of Baseball Prospectus.*

Index of Names

Abreu, Bryan 50, 98
Adolph, Ross 91, 107
Altuve, José 20
Alvarez, Yordan 22
Armenteros, Rogelio 52, 100
Barber, Colin 91
Biagini, Joe 54
Bielak, Brandon 92, 103
Brantley, Michael 24
Bregman, Alex 26
Brewer, Jordan 91, 104
Brown, Hunter 92
Castellanos, Humberto 92
Conine, Brett 92
Correa, Carlos 28
Dawson, Ronnie 91, 106
Deason, Cody 92
Deetz, Dean 92
Devenski, Chris 56
Díaz, Aledmys 30
Emanuel, Kent 92
Garneau, Dustin 32
Greinke, Zack 58
Gurriel, Yuli 34
Henley, Blair 107
Hughes, Jared 60
Ivey, Tyler 92, 104
James, Josh 62
Javier, Cristian 92, 101
Jones, Taylor 91
Kessinger, Grae 91, 105
Lee, Korey 91, 99
Maldonado, Martín 36
Martes, Francis 87
Matijevic, J.J. 91, 106
Mayfield, Jack 38
McCullers Jr., Lance 88
McHugh, Collin 64
Nova, Freudis 91, 101
Osuna, Roberto 66
Paredes, Enoli 92
Peacock, Brad 68
Pena, Jeremy 91, 97
Pérez, Cionel 89
Pressly, Ryan 70
Pruitt, Austin 72
Reddick, Josh 40
Rivera, Jose Alberto 92, 105
Rodriguez, Nivaldo 92
Sanchez, Aaron 74
Santana, Luis 91, 105
Schroeder, Jayson 92
Smith, Joe 76
Sneed, Cy 78
Solis, Jairo 102
Solomon, Peter 92
Springer, George 42
Straw, Myles 44, 103
Stubbs, Garrett 86, 104
Taylor, Blake 92
Toro, Abraham 46, 98
Tucker, Kyle 48

Houston Astros 2020

Urquidy, Jose 80, 96
Valdez, Framber 82
Verlander, Justin 84
Whitley, Forrest 90, 95